THE CHURCH FACES THE WORLD

Late New Testament Writings

WESTMINSTER GUIDES TO THE BIBLE

Edwin M. Good, General Editor

THE CHURCH
FACES
THE WORLD

Late New Testament Writings

by
J. CHRISTIAAN BEKER

Philadelphia
THE WESTMINSTER PRESS

PRINTED IN THE UNITED STATES OF AMERICA

Contents

Contents

Preface

THE church is always "facing the world." In the other volumes on the New Testament in this series, we see how the church faced the world with the gospel of Christ. In this book, the problem is different. For here, Dr. Beker is showing us how the early church began to face the questions and pressures that the world threw up to it. And in facing them, the church had also to come to terms with itself.

In a very real way, this book comes closer to us in the contemporary church than any other book in the series. In the period after the death of the first generation of Christians, the problems that have plagued us ever since came first to the fore. They are *our* problems. For we too must consider, as they did, how to understand the non-Christian world of nations and cultures from the vantage point of faith and the gospel. We too must wrestle with serious questions of belief and right doctrine. We too must decide how the church can live on in the world and, at the same time, can maintain the urgency of its message as the proclamation of God's own world, which overrides this one. These problems faced Christians of the period in this book; they still rise up, clamoring for our answer.

So the subjects of this book are much like us. Yet the reader will find their familiarity in a new way. Books like James and I Peter, which he may have considered simple enough, will

7

take on a new color and a lively complexity. Books like Revelation, which he thought too complicated, will take on a new simplicity. But through them all, the reader will find his own problems and those of his church coming to light.

The Westminster Guides to the Bible grew in the first instance out of the stimulus of the Layman's Theological Library. If, we thought, laymen in the church could be so eloquently encouraged to be theologians, why could they not be encouraged to be Biblical scholars as well? In the modern resurgence of serious thinking about the Christian faith, the study of the Bible has played a major role. But the methods and results of this recent study have not been made available to laymen.

The Westminster Guides to the Bible seek to fill this gap. In nine brief volumes, we introduce the riches of the major portions of the Bible and of the period "between the Testaments." The writers share the conviction that the Bible lies at the heart of Christianity, and that it is imperative that laymen be aided to take a firm grip on Biblical faith. We are certain that this means no denial of the mind. On the contrary, the Bible demands the utmost our minds can give it, and searching study repays our efforts with new insight.

Of course, we are primarily concerned with the Bible, not with our books about it. We hope that the reader will have his Bible in hand as he reads these books, and that he will turn to it again with greater anticipation when he has finished.

And it is with laymen, who are the backbone of the church, that we are concerned. We have written, not for scholars already learned, but for those who seek to learn. We are certain that no wishy-washy faith, no cheap "religiousness," is wanted. In the vigor of Biblical faith we trust that the reader will find invigoration. If so, the church of Christ will be served.

EDWIN M. GOOD

CHAPTER 1 | *The Word and the World*

CHRISTIANITY is a religion that takes history seriously. It proclaims that God involves himself in the concrete historical lives of people. This proclamation stems from the conviction that God has revealed himself decisively in the historical person of Jesus Christ, who lived, died, and rose at a specific place and in a specific time in history. The New Testament is the only reliable witness we possess with regard to the person of Jesus Christ and God's action in him for the salvation of mankind. Those who believe this constitute the people of God, and it is with the people of God in a specific time in history that we are here concerned.

It is our task to let them come alive, to show the situations in which they found themselves — the cultural, political, and religious conditions of their time. And we must show how in that time they reacted to the message of salvation that had become the cornerstone of their lives. Only when we understand the problems, the faith, and the hope of these people in their situation, can God's word to them become alive for us. Only then do we discover that their situation, so different from ours in many respects, calls forth expectations and problems that are as much ours as theirs. Unless we can see the word of God as it came into that particular past period of history, the New Testament, which witnesses to the power of that word, remains a closed book for us.

9

The literature we shall deal with comprises the last twelve books of the New Testament, which came out of the decades after Paul's death. Traditionally, this literature is divided into the following sections: three Pastoral Epistles (I and II Timothy, Titus); seven Catholic Epistles (James; I and II Peter; I, II, and III John; and Jude); The Letter to the Hebrews; and The Revelation. The name "Pastoral" designates letters that deal with advice from one pastor to other pastors. The name "Catholic" was given those writings addressed to the whole, that is, "catholic," church rather than to specific churches or persons. The Catholic Epistles were supposed to have been written by the apostles whose names they bear. The Pastoral Epistles and Hebrews were attributed to the apostle Paul; and The Revelation, to the apostle John.

All the writings have one feature in common. Each is in letter form, whether it actually is a letter or not. The letter form became the predominant way of Christian writing after Paul had made it the popular means of communicating the Christian message. After Paul's death his letters were collected and published. This had a great influence on the pattern of subsequent Christian writing. For example, Hebrews tries to be a letter but sounds much more like a sermon; and The Revelation is prefaced by seven letters to the churches of Asia but is actually a prophetic vision.

A more important common mark of these writings is that they all share a concern for the place of the church in the midst of an ongoing world. However strange this may seem to us, the ongoing world constituted a problem for the faith and life of the early Christians. Before discussing the writings individually, let us look at the first-century world and the place of the church in it.

THE WORLD AROUND THE CHURCH

In A.D. 68 Nero, the fifth Roman emperor, committed suicide, after a fourteen-year reign of blood, and plunged Italy and the provinces into a new civil war. Nero's reign (A.D. 54–68) was characterized by irresponsible despotism and extravagances of all kinds. The image of such a man stays alive for a long time. Not only did he sing a song of the burning of Troy while Rome went up in flames before his eyes; he also murdered his mother and later his wife in a gruesome way. His self-esteem did not suffer at all, for on his deathbed he exclaimed, "What an artist dies with me!" Yet the book of The Revelation will pick up the image of Nero and describe him as the beast, the supreme evil in history (Rev., ch. 13). It was Nero who instigated the first persecution of Christians in Rome in seeking a scapegoat for the fire of Rome, which destroyed three fourths of the city. The fire was rumored to have been a crime of Nero himself.

However, a picture of all Roman emperors as immoral criminals and madmen, who thought themselves to be gods and persecuted Christians systematically, is a generalization that does not stand up under scrutiny. The personal lives of many emperors were marked by cruelty and despotism, but the administration of the huge Roman Empire was carried out by most of them with amazing concern for justice. In fact, the emperors may be called "Empire builders," so effective was their policy of centralization, of control over the courts and over the governors of the provinces. A good example of this is to be found in the correspondence of Pliny, the governor of Bithynia in Asia Minor, with the Emperor Trajan in A.D. 112. Pliny asked for instructions about many matters concerning the administration and welfare of the province, and he received at every occasion a personal answer from the emperor himself.

The fairness of the imperial administration came to light especially under the Flavians, the emperors who succeeded Nero: Vespasian (A.D. 69–79), the military commander of the Oriental legions, famous for his suppression of the Jewish rebellion; and Titus (A.D. 79–81), who succeeded Vespasian in the East and conquered Jerusalem in A.D. 70.

Domitian (A.D. 81–96) interrupted the series of " good " emperors. His open defiance of all legal institutions, his public desire to be called *Dominus et Deus* (Lord and God), and his arbitrary persecution of any person or group that he suspected were passionately condemned by the author of the book of The Revelation. Nor was he tolerated by Roman society. This " revived Nero " was murdered in A.D. 96 and promptly condemned by the Roman senate. He was succeeded by a long line of just, often harsh, but popular emperors who led the Roman Empire into its Golden Age. They were: Nerva (A.D. 96–98), Trajan (98–117), Hadrian (117–138), Antoninus Pius (138–161), and the Stoic philosopher, Marcus Aurelius (161–180).

The person of the emperor represented the unity of the vast Roman Empire with its variety of peoples and races. Allegiance to the state was the life nerve of the Empire, and the role of traditional Roman religion was marked by this practical-political interest. Since the gods were primarily state gods, it was principally in his political function that the emperor received divine honors. This deification of the emperor was the East's legacy to Rome, for the Near Eastern concept of the divine king was transferred from native rulers to the Roman emperors when they conquered the East.

The imperial administration was tolerant of national and religious customs in the Eastern provinces. We know that the Jews were granted privileges that enabled them to live according to their law. As long as the political unity of the Empire was not threatened, tolerance was the mark of the *Pax Romana* (the Roman era of peace). However, the church separated itself from Judaism and its privileges and was recognized as an entity in itself. The church's primary allegiance to the eternal Lord of creation and history rather than to the Roman emperor, the temporary lord of the world, was the source of the struggle between the church and the Empire.

THE CONCERNS OF THE CHURCH

Paul's career was over. He had become a martyr for the Christian cause. But the consequences of his career were lasting. He was, as no other, responsible for the spread of the Christian faith beyond its Palestinian confines into the Gentile world. Indeed, Christianity was now largely a faith for the Gentiles. The struggle with Judaism, which had been such an intense problem for Paul, had ended in the victory of the Gentile mission. The fall of Jerusalem in A.D. 70 spelled the decline of the Jewish wing of the Christian church. Henceforth, Jewish Christianity was to be a sect on the periphery of the Christian movement. The future belonged to Gentile Christianity.

As it expanded in the Gentile world, Christianity encountered a variety of peoples and thought. The most flourishing center of Christian activity was Asia Minor, to which most of the literature with which we are concerned was addressed. R. M. Grant, describing the church in the second century, has said: " The writers of Rome are distinguished from the others by their practical spirit, by their sense of responsibility, by the firmness of their moral concern. The Egyptians, more idealistic, attempt vast syntheses; they try to explain the world or at least to give general pictures of Christian teaching. The Asiatics hold above all to the transmission of the tradition they have received from the apostles and struggle with an invincible firmness against heresies. Finally, the Syrians and the Palestinians usually become chroniclers or historians, unless they draw up codes of liturgy or morals."

The common heritage. What is the tie that binds these churches, located in such different locales and reacting in such different ways to the word of the gospel and to the world around them? It is a common heritage, received from the missionaries and apostles, which begins to be crystallized into statements in which the believer confesses his faith in Christ. These statements, like the one to which Paul refers in I Cor. 12:3, " Jesus is Lord," finally developed into the creeds of the church. One development reached the form that we know as The Apostles' Creed. It goes back to the baptismal creed of the church in Rome around A.D. 150. In the Pastoral Epistles we sometimes come across such embryo creeds in the context of preaching or teaching, for example, I Tim. 3:16. Again in I Peter 1:18-20: " You know that you were ransomed from the futile ways inherited from your fathers, . . . with the precious blood of Christ, like that of a lamb without blemish or spot. *He was destined before the foundation of the world but was made manifest at the end of the times for your sake.*"

This quotation also shows that this generation inherited a tradition stamped by hope in the final arrival of the Kingdom of God ushered in by the resurrection of Christ. The appearance of Jesus Christ marks " the end of the times." In this sense, Paul had spoken about Christians " upon whom the end of the ages has come " (I Cor. 10:11). He had admonished them that " the appointed time has grown very short; from now on, let those who have wives live as though they had none, and those who mourn as though they were not mourning, and those who rejoice as though they were not rejoicing, and those who buy as though they had no goods, and those who deal with the world as though they had no dealings with it. For the form of this world is passing away " (I Cor. 7:29-31). Faith in Christ meant belief in the nearness of the end of the world and the arrival of the Kingdom of God. This was the heritage that the church had received from the apostles, and this bound its members together and marked their lives.

Consolidation and adaptation. This central theme of hope evoked the concerns of this period. The Return of Christ seemed delayed, but the hope of the Second Coming remained. This hope was expressed in Greek by the term *parousia.* (I Cor. 15:23; James 5:7; II Peter 1:16; 3:4, 12; I John 2:28.) Technically it means the arrival of an emperor in a city, but the Christians used the term for the expected glorious arrival of their King, Jesus Christ. But the *Parousia,* still expected by Paul in his own lifetime (I Cor. 15:51), was not forthcoming, and the world did not pass away. How then did the church maintain the message of hope in an ongoing world? This is the central question in this literature, for the church had to come to terms with the affairs of the world and yet safeguard its identity. How did it react to this disappointed expectation? Did it give up its hope completely? Was it swallowed up within the secular institutions of the Roman Empire? If not, how did it react to the Roman Empire? How could the church be in the world but not of the world?

The search for self-identity manifested itself in the church's growing liturgy, doctrine, and ethics. A need for stability was felt. The church began to organize itself. It would be wrong to say that the church suddenly surrendered its life in hope and its enthusiastic, spontaneous witness of the Spirit and became merely an institution. Yet a transition became gradually visible, which, after the close of the period covered by the New Testament books, gained in force until it finally reached its fulfillment in the institution of the early Catholic Church. Even now the transition from the early church, which was guided immediately by the Holy Spirit, into the early Catholic Church, in which the Spirit was channeled into distinct patterns of office, was under way in certain forms of the life of the church. The development can be seen especially in the Pastoral Epistles. Stabilization of belief and worship was a necessity if the church was to safeguard its unity, and forms of organization were the outward expression of this unity. In the noncanonical literature of the period, which is called the " Apostolic Fathers," we observe a similar growth of organizational patterns. The letters of Ignatius, Bishop of Antioch (about A.D. 115), already revealed a pattern in which one bishop expressed the visible unity of the church.

In other areas the early Christian hope in the imminent coming of God's Kingdom was reaffirmed. In fact, one of the surprising elements in this literature is that, notwithstanding an awareness of having to come to terms with the world, the Christian hope remained a central feature. Some writers stressed it more than others. The Pastor's emphasis was quite different from that of the writer of the book of Revelation, but the consciousness of living in the last times never faded. It was the result of a conviction that the love of God in Christ would be the ultimate factor that would judge the world.

THE CHURCH IS THREATENED

However, the church's search for self-identity was now accompanied by movements that threatened to destroy it. There was both a danger from within and a danger from without.

The danger from within. The attempt to express Christian beliefs in terms of outward organization inevitably created different viewpoints. Orthodoxy always has its traveling companion, heresy. This was true from the very beginning of the church. Even Paul had to struggle with those who were caus-

ing schisms and heresies in his churches. The word "orthodoxy" comes from a Greek term, and it means "correct"
(*ortho*) "opinion" (*doxa*). In church usage it finally came to
mean the body of correct doctrines. Although the term itself
is absent from the New Testament, Gal. 2:14 and II Tim. 2:15
point to it. "Heresy" originally meant in Greek simply an
"opinion" or a "party," often referring to the tenets of certain
philosophic schools without any negative meaning. Thus Jo-
sephus, the Jewish historian, describes the parties of the Jews
— the Pharisees, the Sadducees, and the Essenes — as *haireseis*,
Greek for "heresies." Likewise, Paul in Acts 24:14 states that
he belongs to a certain *hairesis* among the Jews, by which he
meant the Christian party. However, already in I Cor. 11:19,
Paul uses the word in a derogatory sense. From the time of the
Pastoral Epistles it is used to designate theological error (see
II Peter 2:1; Titus 3:10). Heresy, then, is an interpretation of
Christian faith that is built on false presumptions. The early
church often denounced it in such terms as adultery, because
the heretic adhered to principles that were judged faithless to
the church.

The question was: Who would provide the correct interpretation of Christian faith? Who was the orthodox and who
the heretic? On what basis could the church decide? In this
period, we can observe the development of the norms of the
Christian faith based on the confession of Christ. For example,
there was a movement toward a collection of normative writings, the canon. There were correct and incorrect stories and
traditions about Jesus Christ and the Christian faith, and some
choice had to be made. Heresy not only brought in dangerous
notions but also split the unity of the church and tried to dis-
solve it.

Later we shall investigate types of heresy and their tenets.
Let it be stressed here how unclear the boundaries between

heresy and orthodoxy often were. It is difficult for us to know
the case for the heretics since the church has destroyed all their
literature. We know of them only through the denunciations
of the church leaders. It is therefore hazardous to identify the
heretical movements. The early church did not often debate
with the heretics: it denounced them. We see this clearly in
Jude and II Peter, where abusive language abounds in such a
way that we cannot precisely identify the beliefs of their opponents. But elsewhere, for example in the letters of John,
such identifications can be made. There the heretics adhered to
the conviction that Christ was the Son of God but had not
really appeared in the flesh. On earth the divine substance had
only seemingly a body. We shall see that the heretics of this
period were not Jews but Gentile Christians with leanings toward Judaism or toward forms of Greek religious philosophy.
The struggle with heresy intensified in this period and climaxed in the fierce struggles of the church with Gnosticism in
the second and third centuries. A stabilization of doctrine set
in by the fourth and fifth century: first, with the formulation
of the doctrine of the Trinity at the Council of Nicaea (A.D.
325); and, second, with that of the relation between the divine
and human natures of Christ at the Council of Chalcedon
(A.D. 450).

The danger from without. The danger from without involved the problem of the relation of Christians to non-Chris-
tians, of Christianity to Roman society and to the Roman Empire. The church as a self-conscious movement tried to find a
place within the world. It was threatened not only by forces
from within but also by forces from without, which would
finally attempt to crush it. This clash was created by the problem of allegiance to a national structure, and by the misunder-
standings that were involved in it. In this period, however,
no official persecutions occurred. The word " official " should

be stressed. We must avoid quick generalizations about the persecutions. The first *official* persecutions did not take place until the middle of the third century, in the time of the Emperors Decius (249–51) and Diocletian (284–305).

To be sure, persecutions did occur before this, but they were local in character and were not organized on an Empire-wide basis. They arose because of public pressure and hatred against the movement, and because of the lack of legal status for the church. So long as the Christians were regarded as a " sect," a *halakah,* or " way," within Judaism, they shared the privileges granted to Judaism by the Roman Empire. But after Nero's persecution of Christians in Rome in connection with the fire, and especially after the fall of Jerusalem in A.D. 70, it became increasingly clear that Christianity was a new religion, endangering the security of the state by refusing to pay divine honors to the emperor. The Roman historian Tacitus, writing about A.D. 110, spoke of the Christians as " the hated of the human race."

Public gossip, rumors, and deprecations were the first persecutions Christians had to suffer. They were held in suspicion because of their refusal to participate in Roman national life, because of their denial of the gods and the cults, and because of their secret meetings in which all sorts of crimes were supposed to take place. The authorities were at first unwilling to take serious measures, but public pressure and denunciations of Christians forced them to investigate the principles of the movement. The test was loyalty to the state, expressed in sacrificing to the gods and paying honor to the emperor. Because of Christian refusal to do these things, the road to official persecution was opened.

A Word on Procedure

We shall look at these books according to the themes touched upon above: (1) the people of God in search of self-identity: efforts of consolidation; (2) the people of God threatened from within: the danger of heresy; (3) the people of God threatened from without: the danger of public opinion and the state.

Although the New Testament writings that we shall consider touch on several or all of those topics, the division should clarify the central themes. Chapters 2 and 3 treat the Pastoral Epistles and James, respectively, with the theme of the search for self-identity. Chapters 4 and 5 deal with the threat from within the church when treating Hebrews and five of the Catholic Epistles. Finally, Chapters 6 and 7 consider the threat from without and the relation of Christianity to public opinion and the state, as expressed in I Peter and The Revelation.

| *Advice for Ministers*

THE earliest days of Christian enthusiasm were over. A transition period had set in, in which people began to wonder about their former expectation of the nearness of God's Kingdom. The kingdom of the Roman emperor seemed more manifest than the Kingdom of God. Hope in the speedy advent of the Kingdom of God had characterized the apostolic message. What was to become of this expectation after the apostles died, and after it had become clear that the church would have to continue to live within the world? How would the church maintain its message of hope in an ongoing world? It must come to terms with the world and yet be distinct from it.

Furthermore, new converts were added to the church who had not shared the time of apostolic fervor and who brought new and strange interpretations to bear upon the faith and apostolic tradition. Coupled with this went the disquieting experience that belonging to the church made one suspect in the eyes of the world. And yet the church had to come to terms with the world because the hope in the imminent arrival of God's world had been a disappointment. Amidst these dangers from within and without, the Pastoral Epistles (I and II Timothy and Titus) illustrate how the church went about adjusting itself to the new conditions.

The name " Pastoral " suggests what the letters themselves

indicate — that a pastor is writing to pastors about the problems of their churches. The churches addressed are located in Asia Minor, Paul's former missionary territory. After the fall of Jerusalem in A.D. 70, Asia Minor with its capital, Ephesus, had become the stronghold of the Christian movement. The book of The Revelation addresses letters to seven Christian churches there, and so does the second-century bishop, Ignatius of Antioch. In a time when the authority of the apostle Paul was used for the wrong ends by heretics in the church, an admirer of Paul chose the letter form to admonish and direct these churches in Asia Minor. He wrote in a way Paul would have written were he alive, and he may even have possessed certain fragments of Paul's correspondence, which he incorporated in his epistles. If anywhere, this has occurred in II Timothy, the most Pauline and personal among the letters. (See II Tim. 4:9-18.) Furthermore, he not only imitated Paul's method of writing, but, what is more significant, he also adopted Paul's authority, to strengthen the appeal of his writings. Why would he have done so? We must recognize, first of all, how important the question of authority became in the era after the death of the apostles. They had been living witnesses to the risen Lord and had personally received the Apostolic Commission from him. Their authority in deciding issues of faith and morals was gone, and the question of their successors was bound to arise. The longer the expected Return of the Lord delayed, the more urgent became this question.

No wonder, then, that with the death of the original witnesses the need for reliable tradition about Christ became exceedingly important. In connection with this came the question of who would safeguard this tradition and keep it pure from false interpretations by heretics until such time as the Lord would return. The need for " sound doctrine " as the foundation for the ongoing life of the church, in order "to confute those who contradict it" (Titus 1:9), comes to the fore in the Pastorals. The disrupting influences of the heretics and efforts toward consolidating the church in opposition to them are basic themes in the Pastoral Epistles.

THE NATURE OF THE HERETICS

Although the character of heresy will be discussed later with greater detail, the interrelatedness of the literature of this era does not permit us to be silent about the subject here. In fact, the efforts of the Pastor will be understood only if they are seen against the background of heretical inroads into the life of the church. The heretics were not outsiders but flourished in the midst of the church and seem to have had considerable success. "Their [the heretics'] talk will eat its way like gangrene." (II Tim. 2:17.) The author put prophecies about the end of time in the mouth of Paul to let his readers know that what "Paul" prophesied was a fact: "Now the Spirit expressly says that in later times some will depart from the faith by giving heed to deceitful spirits and doctrines of demons" (I Tim. 4:1). Again: "For the time is coming when people will not endure sound teaching, but having itching ears they will accumulate for themselves teachers to suit their own likings, and will turn away from listening to the truth and wander into myths." (II Tim. 4:3-4.)

When we inquire about these myths or about the precise character of this heresy, we find only vague allusions. Two characteristics stand out: asceticism and spiritualism. Asceticism, self-denial for religious purposes, manifests itself in the prohibition of marriage (I Tim. 4:3; see also chs. 2:15; 5:14; Titus 2:4) and in abstinence from certain foods (I Tim. 4:3; 5:23). These ascetic features arise from the conviction that crea-

tion and procreation are essentially harmful to salvation and
that salvation consists in avoiding contact with an evil and corrupt world. In contrast to their negative view of matter, they
exalt the soul. Secret knowledge about heavenly realms, speculation and excitement about a spiritual life that disregards the
body, lead to the conviction that the God of redemption is not
the God of creation. This implies that salvation is only for the
soul of man, not for the whole person. The church countered
by insisting that the God of redemption was also the God of
creation (I Tim. 4:4). The heretics believed that a consequence
of Jesus' resurrection and ascension from earth to heaven was
that their own lives in Christ had already been transported to
a heavenly existence (II Tim. 2:18). These were the beginnings
of a prominent heresy, Gnosticism (a word derived from the
Greek word *gnosis,* meaning " mysterious knowledge "), which
will be discussed in Chapter 5. In this regard, Timothy must
" avoid the godless chatter and contradictions of what is falsely
called knowledge " (I Tim. 6:20).

The Church's Reaction

How does the Pastor handle these heretical teachings? He
behaved very much like some of us, who, when questioned on
points of faith, cut short all discussion by pronouncing that if
one doesn't believe this or that, one cannot call himself a Christian. Although a bishop must be able " to confute those who
contradict it [sound doctrine] " (Titus 1:9), the Pastor himself
seemed to equate confutation with renunciation. Indeed, the
Pastor was not interested in a description of the heretics or in
a debate about the questions involved. He was concerned not
to argue with heresy but to exterminate it. The fact of heresy
threatened the unity of the church. That was enough cause to
condemn it. And he proceeded to lambaste his opponents in the
most general terms:

" For there are many insubordinate men, empty talkers and deceivers, especially the circumcision party; they must be silenced, since they are upsetting whole families by teaching for base gain what they have no right to teach. One of themselves, a prophet of their own, said, 'Cretans are always liars, evil beasts, lazy gluttons.' " (Titus 1:10-12.)

"To the pure all things are pure, but to the corrupt and unbelieving nothing is pure; their very minds and consciences are corrupted. . . . They are detestable, disobedient, unfit for any good deed." (Titus 1:15-16; see I Tim. 1:3-11; 4:1-5; II Tim. 3:1-9.)

We shall see later that this method of attack was in accordance with the trend of the times, especially the equation of heresy with adultery and fornication. This originated from the Old Testament prophetic denunciation of "whoring after gods of the strangers." The method is deplorable perhaps, but it clarifies two issues. The first is that the substitution of denunciation for debate reveals the church's inability to deal with the issue successfully. It points to the earliest beginnings of controversy, in which the church had not yet formulated a way of dealing with these questions. Furthermore, the language of abuse shows that the church could not afford an academic debate at this particular time. Its very existence as the church of Jesus Christ was at stake. And the unity of the church was the greater issue, which made even these weapons of poverty a necessity.

We must recognize that the church had a correct intuition about the extreme danger the heretics constituted in its midst. The life-and-death struggle of the church with Gnosticism in the second and third centuries had its beginnings here. The

Pastor felt correctly that tolerance for such ideas would mean the end of the Gospel. The Gnostics' way of thinking was described by the Pastor as occupation " with myths and endless genealogies which promote speculations rather than the divine training that is in faith " (I Tim. 1:4). Therefore, the Pastor stressed the virtues of everyday decency. What has often been called the bourgeois, middle-class ethic of the Pastorals — " sobriety " (Titus 2:12), " a godly life " (I Tim. 2:2; Titus 2:12), and being " well thought of by outsiders " (I Tim. 3:7) — became important in the struggle against the ecstasies and peculiarities of the heretics. The healthy emphasis on the concreteness of earthly life served a similar purpose. The gifts of creation were appreciated. " For everything created by God is good, and nothing is to be rejected if it is received with thanksgiving; for then it is consecrated by the word of God and prayer " (I Tim. 4:4-5). Against the spiritualistic abstinence of his opponents, he advised that one should enjoy " a little wine " (ch. 5:23) and that having children is the proper business for women (ch. 2:15).

The ethic of decency was not just a weapon against the heretics. It also served the policy of the church with respect to the outside world. The Christians were subjects of gossip and slander. " Public relations " became a matter of some importance. Therefore, aspirants for the office of bishop " must be well thought of by outsiders " and their families must be of good repute (ch. 3:1-7). The Pastor urged: " Show yourself in all respects a model of good deeds, and in your teaching show integrity, gravity, and sound speech that cannot be censured, so that an opponent may be put to shame, having nothing evil to say of us." (Titus 2:7-8.) The fact that Christians were a peculiar people among the peoples of the world did not mean an ostentatious peculiarity. " Remind them to be submissive to rulers and authorities, to be obedient, to be ready

for any honest work, to speak evil of no one, to avoid quarreling, to be gentle and to show perfect courtesy toward all men."
(Ch. 3:1-2.)

THE CHURCH'S UPBUILDING

At the same time that the church was counteracting the
heretics within and courting public opinion without, it had to
determine its own position. The Pastoral Epistles deal with
three areas of concern in which the church was consolidating
itself: tradition, worship, and administration. With these letters we are in the midst of a period of transition. Because we
have so little information about the period, we constantly run
the risk of exaggerating its trends. Trends, after all, are not
fixed patterns: they are movements. Everything was in motion.
The church still had a long way to go before reaching the early
Catholic Church's organization, which did not attain a fixed
form until the time of Irenaeus, the bishop of Lyon at the end
of the second century. In the meantime, no straight line of
development can be assumed. Differing forms of liturgy and
administrative practice were prevalent in the various provinces
of the Roman Empire where churches existed.

The tradition. The Pastor pointed regularly to the foundation of the church's life: " Guard the truth that has been entrusted to you " (II Tim. 1:14; see also I Tim. 6:20); " follow
the pattern of the sound words which you have heard from
me " (II Tim. 1:13); deacons must hold " the mystery of the
faith " (I Tim. 3:9); heretics " are upsetting the faith " (II
Tim. 2:18); and heretics have departed " from the faith "
(I Tim. 4:1).

" Faith " for the Pastor had become the formulation of the
apostolic tradition. When we compare the vitality of Paul's
statements about faith, the urgency and directness of his religious appeal, with that of the Pastor, we must be struck by

the shift that has occurred. The character of faith as personal surrender to, and trust in, the living Lord has undergone a shift to a more intellectual emphasis. Faith is in the process of becoming *the* faith, a body of Christian convictions to which assent is required. This tendency must not be exaggerated. Christian faith is always focused upon God's action in Christ. Paul also spoke about "the faith" (Rom. 1:5). Without it Christianity could not have become a religion distinct from Judaism with a missionary impulse of its own. And yet the personal realism of Paul's witness is no longer present.

A similar shift took place in the realm of ethics. Just as "the faith" was the necessary norm by which heresy was judged, so a code of ethics was necessary, as we have seen, against the world-denying heretics. In this process, however, a new danger had crept in. The antithesis in Paul between faith and the law was no longer felt. The Christian way of life could no longer be stated in terms of guidance by the Spirit of Christ. Something more specific was needed. And so it happened that Paul's struggle against the law ceased to be understood, and the law entered the church again, albeit in a new guise. This new guise was a noble ethic for humanity, decency, and godliness. Words rarely found in Paul's letters show this tendency toward a middle-class ethic of decency. "The grace of God has appeared . . . training us to renounce irreligion and worldly passions and to live sober, upright, and godly lives in this world." (Titus 2:11-12.) "The sound words of our Lord Jesus Christ and the teaching which accords with godliness" (I Tim. 6:3) are with "good deeds" (Titus 3:8) and "a good conscience" (I Tim. 1:5, 19; see also ch. 3:9; II Tim. 1:3) the model for the Christian.

The Liturgy. The consolidation of the content of faith in confessional formulations is apparent in the Pastoral Epistles.

Again and again fragments of hymns, bits of liturgical formulas, and credal catchwords are incorporated in the Pastor's admonitions. We can observe how the church is gradually formulating its liturgy. For example: " To the King of ages, immortal, invisible, the only God, be honor and glory for ever and ever. Amen." (I Tim. 1:17.) Also: " The blessed and only Sovereign, the King of kings and Lord of lords, who alone has immortality and dwells in unapproachable light, whom no man has ever seen or can see. To him be honor and eternal dominion. Amen." (I Tim. 6:15-16; see Titus 2:13.)

Likewise, sentences appear that were used for instruction of new converts. Such instruction was required for admission to the church and formed the basis for the baptismal confessions. Often liturgical pieces are introduced by the formula " the saying is sure," and close with the admonition to " insist " on these essentials in teaching. For example: " The saying is sure:

If we have died with him, we shall also live with him;
if we endure, we shall also reign with him;
if we deny him, he also will deny us;
if we are faithless, he remains faithful —

for he cannot deny himself. Remind them of this." (II Tim. 2:11-14; see also I Tim. 1:15; 3:1; 4:9; Titus 3:8.)

The beginnings of credal forms also appear frequently. We can detect something of the process that leads from the earliest creed in Paul's, " Jesus is Lord " (I Cor. 12:3), to what we know in our churches as the Apostles' Creed, based on the baptismal confession of the church at Rome at the end of the second century. The statement, " Jesus is Lord," seems to have been gradually expanded. First, the confession of Christ has been made more explicit: " Great indeed, we confess, is the mystery of our religion:

> " He was manifested in the flesh,
>   vindicated in the Spirit,
>   seen by angels,
>   preached among the nations,
>   believed on in the world,
>   taken up in glory."
>
> (I Tim. 3:16.)

Then the confession to God the Father was placed in front of it: " For there is one God, and there is one mediator between God and men, the man Christ Jesus, who gave himself as a ransom for all " (I Tim. 2:5); and, " In the presence of God who gives life to all things, and of Christ Jesus who in his testimony before Pontius Pilate made the good confession " (I Tim. 6:13). Finally, the third article, the confession of the Holy Spirit, emerged. Paul formulates it in II Cor. 13:14, and it takes this form in Titus 3:4-8: " But when the goodness and loving kindness of God our Savior appeared, he saved us, . . . by the washing of regeneration and renewal in the Holy Spirit, which he poured out upon us richly through Jesus Christ our Savior, so that we might be justified by his grace and become heirs in hope of eternal life. The saying is sure."

The formulation of the liturgy is accompanied by a growing concern for worship. In the Pastorals we find one of the earliest rules for the conduct of worship, that is, the order of prayer and the way men and women must behave and dress in the church. " I urge that supplications, prayers, intercessions, and thanksgivings be made for all men, . . . that in every place the men should pray, lifting holy hands without anger or quarreling; also that women should adorn themselves modestly and sensibly in seemly apparel." (I Tim. 2:1, 8-9.) The growing regulation in the order of worship becomes apparent when we compare it with the earliest type of Christian worship reflected in I Cor., ch. 14. The earliest Christian congregation was a gathering directly guided by the Spirit. "When you come together, each one has a hymn, a lesson, a revelation, a tongue, or an interpretation." (V. 26.) Leadership was in the hands of the prophets. This was an undefined office, for anyone could aspire to prophecy (v. 39). The boundary between prophecy and speaking in "tongues" (ecstatic, unintelligible utterances) was ill-defined. I Corinthians, ch. 14, shows the attempts of Paul to safeguard both the freedom of the Spirit ("desire the spiritual gifts, especially that you may prophesy") and the order of the service ("God is not a God of confusion but of peace"). Disorder must have occurred at the celebration of the Eucharist, for Paul blames some for behaving as undignified egotists (I Cor. 11:20-22). The need for order and form drove the church to apply more rigidly the Jewish pattern of worship, which it had already adopted. Such is the situation the Pastorals present.

Administration. The selection of the clergy was an important matter for the Pastor. He gave directives for administration and laid down the conditions for those aspiring to become bishops (I Tim., chs. 3; 4:12 to 5:22; Titus 1:5-9). The clergy was crucial in the church's search for self-identity. Leadership must be strong and reliable if the church intended to combat heresy and seek for some understanding with the world.

The death of the apostles had been a severe blow to the church. As men commissioned by the risen Lord himself, they had exercised a decisive voice in church affairs. But who was to take over their authority? We have seen how important it was for the church to have a reliable tradition about Christ against the speculations of the heretics. The heretics, however, often used the same tradition of the faith but interpreted it falsely. A need arose for correct interpreters. This was to be the function of the clergy. A duly appointed clergy must hand down reliable, that is, apostolic, tradition. In this light we understand the Pastor's repeated admonitions: " O Timothy, guard what has been entrusted to you. Avoid the godless chatter and contradictions of what is falsely called knowledge " (I Tim. 6:20); " Continue in what you have learned and have firmly believed, knowing from whom you learned it " (II Tim. 3:14).

At the time of the Pastoral Epistles, the early second century A.D., the church was formulating an apostolic tradition along with reliable interpreters of it. We can see in the Pastorals that the church was groping for an adequate organization. A few words about the growth of the ministry will clarify the stage of development to which the Pastorals belong. From the time of Paul, the interaction of two types of ministry can be discerned. The first is the charismatic or spontaneous type; the second, the regularly appointed type. Paul understood all ministries to be an outpouring of the gift of the Spirit, since all Christians shared the Spirit. To Paul, ministries were not characterized by fixed qualifications or by rites of ordination. " Now there are varieties of gifts, but the same Spirit; and there are varieties of service, but the same Lord; and there are varieties of working, but it is the same God who inspires them all in every one. To each is given the manifestation of the Spirit for the common good." (I Cor. 12:4-7.) It was through the gift of the Spirit alone that prophets, teachers, and evangelists stood out as the leaders of the churches, along with the apostles.

But alongside this charismatic group of ministers, a hint of the later church officials can be discerned. It developed out of certain groups of people to whom a special task was given. I Thessalonians 5:12, for example, exhorts Christians to respect " those who labor among you and are over you in the Lord and admonish you." I Corinthians 16:16 urges the Corinthians " to be subject " to men like Stephanas " and to every fellow worker

and laborer." Within the churches certain tasks had to be dis-
charged and certain financial and business measures taken. It
would be contrary to the evidence to limit the function of the
group to organizational tasks. They had both an administrative
and a pastoral function. But within this group lies the origin
of the three later offices of bishop, presbyter, and deacon. This
may mark the beginning of fixed offices.

In the period of the Pastorals the church was attempting to
strike a balance between the charismatic leader and the appointed administrator. The Pastorals indicate that there is no
strict division between the prophets and the appointed clergy.
They work side by side: "Do not neglect the gift you have,
which was given you by prophetic utterance when the elders
laid their hands upon you" (I Tim. 4:14; see ch. 1:18). With
the delay of the Coming of Christ and the disappearance of the
apostles, the prophetic office began to disintegrate. Furthermore, the rise of false teaching and the propagation of it by
false prophets made prophecy suspect. There followed an attempt to bring the prophets under control and to check their
influence. An early Christian document, the Didache, describes
a situation similar to that of the Pastorals. The Didache sees
a bulwark against heresy in the appointment of worthy bishops
and deacons, "for they also minister to you the ministry of
the prophets and teachers." The Didache implies that if the
bishops and deacons are carefully enough chosen, they will
replace the prophets. This idea is an attempt to put the dangerous aspects of prophecy under the wing of church order. Such
is the situation at the time of the Pastoral Epistles.

However, it is difficult to say whether the threefold pattern
of bishop, elder, and deacon is present in the Pastorals. The
terms " elder " (*presbyteros*) and " bishop " (*episkopos,* which
might also be translated " overseer ") probably refer to the
same office, but come from different traditions. *Episkopos* de-

noted originally a Greco-Roman club official who functioned as the secretary or treasurer. *Presbyteros,* however, came out of the Jewish tradition of " elders " who form the respected council of a community. The word refers primarily to an age group as well as to an official authority. The Pastorals reflect a situation where the office of the overseer or bishop has already emerged out of the group of " men of weight " or elders. The bishop is a distinct leader. The eminence of the office is shown by the careful qualifications that condition eligibility. (See I Tim. 3:1; Titus 1:7-8.)

The Pastorals give the impression of being in the second generation of Christianity, in which the spiritual fire of the apostolic era is being channeled into ecclesiastical forms. A growing institutionalism and a gradual adjustment to the outside world are signs of recognition by the church that it faces a future in society and must come to terms with it. However, the church is conscious of the fact that faithfulness to Christ and the apostolic message entails a price. " Do not be ashamed then of testifying to our Lord, . . . but take your share of suffering for the gospel in the power of God." (II Tim. 1:8.) The church knows that it must suffer and bear abuse for its witness. Co-existence with the world does not mean absorption by the world. The church is therefore prepared to witness for its faith with the witness of life itself (II Tim. 4:6), and the power to do so stems from the conviction: " But I am not ashamed, for I know whom I have believed and I am sure that he is able to guard until that Day what has been entrusted to me " (ch. 1:12).

| *A Manual for the Laity*

THE Letter of James has occupied a disputed place in the history of the Christian church. The early church did not include it easily in the canon of its Scriptures, even at the time of the church father Origen (died A.D. 254). It is well known that Luther characterized James as a "right strawy epistle" and the author as someone who "threw things together in a messy way." Yet, on the other hand, Luther could say: "It seems that James was some good man who obtained some of the words of the apostles' disciples and put them on paper or perhaps someone else made notes on a sermon of his. Therefore I cannot put his among the chief books, but I will not ask anyone else not to, for [the epistle] contains many good sayings."

ORIGIN AND PURPOSE

To be sure, this writing contains "many good sayings" and useful maxims of conduct. One is struck, however, by both the vagueness of historical setting and the lack of Christian emphasis. We do not know when, by whom, or to whom the book was written. We are not even certain that it was intended to be a letter, since it closes abruptly without the customary greetings or personal remarks. There can be no doubt that a Christian wrote the epistle to fellow Christians. He had either the common Christian name, James, or adopted it as if writing in the name of James, the Lord's brother. As The Acts and the Pauline letters indicate, James, the Lord's brother, was the main figure of the Jewish-Christian church in Jerusalem after Peter's departure from that city.

Actually, the author of James may have been less an author than an editor. Many scholars think that he revised and "Christianized" an earlier Jewish treatise on morals for the sake of his fellow Christians, to guide their moral journey through life. This would explain why the epistle has such a Jewish flavor. It would clarify certain sections that make sense only when applied to Jewish life. Furthermore, it would explain the scanty references to Jesus Christ, the Lord of the church.

A small sample of literary analysis as applied to the New Testament will illustrate this point. The opening of the letter (ch. 1:1) shows a working over of an original Jewish greeting: "Jacob [= James], a servant of God to the twelve tribes in the dispersion. Greeting." The Christian editor elaborates this to "James, a servant of God and of the Lord Jesus Christ." This is a unique title in the New Testament. The title "Lord," designating Christ, is found in James only in chs. 2:1 and 5:14. Everywhere else in the letter (eleven times), the word "Lord" refers to God. In ch. 2:1 the Greek text (the RSV smooths it out) reads: "My brethren, show no partiality as you hold the faith of our Lord Jesus Christ of [the] glory." This series of seven words all in the genitive case insert the words Jesus Christ, whereas the original wording was probably the common Jewish expression referring to God as "the Lord of glory." Chapter 2:1-12 dealt in the original source with the behavior toward rich and poor in the synagogue, and was used by James for his Christian purpose.

Some scholars believe that James used as his source a Jewish treatise written in the name of Jacob, which gave moral advice to the Jews of the Dispersion, the world-wide scattering of Jewry since the days of the Babylonian captivity. This was commonly done. The pattern used for such ethical exhortation was taken traditionally from Gen., ch. 49, where Jacob before his death addresses his twelve sons, the twelve tribes of Israel. We know examples of this literary pattern in other Jewish books, such as the Testaments of the Twelve Patriarchs and the works of Philo, the Jewish philosopher. In each case, just as in Gen., ch. 49, each tribe is identified with a vice or virtue. No doubt James employed other sources as well. Jewish materials predominate, especially the thought patterns and style of the Old Testament wisdom literature, and the prophetic and apocalyptic literature (ch. 5:1-6). These are also elements derived from a leading Greek philosophy of the day, that of the Stoics. In ch. 4:1-2, we may almost feel that we are listening to a Stoic preacher, a common figure in market places of the first century. The moral principle that " wars without come from wars within " is very reminiscent of the Stoics, and in v. 3 lust and desire are pointed out as the cause. These are vices that the Stoics emphasized greatly (see also ch. 3:1-12). All these materials seem to have been used, and they are loosely strung together without a very clear pattern or much consistency. Certain sayings stand out in complete isolation, for example, ch. 3:18: " And the harvest of righteousness is sown in peace by those who make peace." This has only the slightest connection with the theme of wisdom at the end of which it occurs (vs. 13-18). Notice also the sayings on swearing and on dedication in ch. 5:12-13.

If we keep the intention of the author in mind, however, it is possible to arrive at a twelvefold division in accordance with the instruction pattern of Gen., ch. 49, and its successors in Jewish literature. James does not address himself to any particular church but to the church universal, to the twelve tribes in the Dispersion, the New Israel. And these twelve tribes are exhorted by twelve different ethical topics, often connected by word associations. For example, the transition from ch. 1:1 to v. 2 in a word play on the Greek verb stem, *char: chairein — chara* (greeting — joy). In vs. 12-13, one Greek word *peirasmos* means both trial (v. 12) and temptation (v. 13), and this leads the author to the next exhortation.

The following outline shows the division of the material into twelve exhortations each devoted to a special concern of the author:

James, to the twelve tribes	ch. 1:1
1. Joy under trial	ch. 1:2-12
2. Every good gift comes from above	ch. 1:13-18
3. " Be doers of the word, and not hearers only "	ch. 1:19-27
4. No partiality between rich and poor	ch. 2:1-13
5. "Faith without works is dead "	ch. 2:14-26
6. " The tongue — a restless evil, full of deadly poison "	
	ch. 3:1-12
7. Avoid false wisdom; choose heavenly wisdom	ch. 3:13-18
8. Avoid false desires; cleanse yourselves	ch. 4:1-12
9. You cannot control the future	ch. 4:13-17
10. Weep and howl, you rich; the judgment is near	ch. 5:1-6
11. Be patient, brethren; the Kingdom is near	ch. 5:7-12
12. The prayer of the righteous man is effective	ch. 5:13-20

The author's purpose. The purpose of the epistle is to strengthen the Christian church on its way from its earthly exile to its heavenly home. The author intends to give a manual to the laity to help it regulate its way of life in the intervening time (ch. 5:8). James has taken the Jewish view of the dispersion of the Jews into the world and interpreted it in the light of the Christian life. It is no longer that people cannot live in the land of their birth and heritage: it is that the church, as the fulfillment of Israel, must live out its life in a spiritual dispersion away from its true home in the Kingdom of God. It must now live in a world alien to its own way of life and dangerous to its existence and destiny. James directs his consolations and exhortation to God's people in the world.

James does not give a theological foundation to the church, for his purpose is pre-eminently practical. He is like many of us who are weary of theological subtleties and decide that the Christian faith is not " talk but walk." Therefore, the author, although himself a teacher, warns against teachers (ch. 3:1-5) and is peculiarly aware of the sins of the tongue (vs. 6-12). For the same reason he distrusts intellectual wisdom as a source of strife and division and defines the wisdom from above as peaceable and gentle (v. 17). To the forces that threatened the people of God belonged also the constant temptation of falling into line with the world (ch. 1:2-3), of kowtowing to the rich (ch. 2:1-2), and of acting as if man were the master of the future (ch. 4:13-14). The " perfect " man is the man of integrity who knows that he lives under God and for God. He does not operate with double standards like the " split soul " (chs. 1:8; 4:8), the schizophrenic who cannot make up his mind whether he belongs to the world or to the Dispersion (the people of God).

We must realize the situation of the first-century church to understand the need for such a manual as James. The church had gone out into the Gentile world and received converts who had not lived under the strong ethics of Judaism. These people had not received adequate moral training and were often perverted by the vices of Roman social life. (See Rom. 1:18-32.) They needed some elementary instruction on the ethical side of the Christian way of life. We find catechetical material of this type in all sections of the New Testament, especially where new moral problems require new solutions.

The author seems to come into his own in the central section of the epistle. His emphases will be most clearly understood if we study chs. 2:1 to 3:12.

WOE TO THE RICH

The author builds on the saying, occurring frequently in Judaism, " God shows no partiality." As a matter of fact, partiality is shown, but it is directed against the wealthy. James was such a zealous defender of the poor that he was prejudiced against the rich and condemned them as a group (chs. 1:11; 2:1-2; 5:1-6). This does not mean that he was an "early Marxist " — against the rich simply because they were rich. He saw the tension between rich and poor as the wisdom writers of the Jews saw it, as a situation in which the rich oppress and the poor are oppressed (see chs. 2:6; 5:1-6). We see here the missionary sentiment of the first century, which found its message rejected by the rich and received primarily by the economically lower groups, as the frequent mention of slaves in the New Testament moral codes indicates.

Moreover, the saying of Jesus in the story of the rich young ruler, " How hard it is for those who have riches to enter the kingdom of God! " (Luke 18:24), is reflected in all subsequent Christian literature. How difficult indeed it was for rich people, who had a solid foundation in this world and had " lived on the earth in luxury and in pleasure " (James 5:5), to take upon themselves the way of the Diaspora, the way of a people alien to this world! It was with this in mind that the Pastor wrote, " For the love of money is the root of all evils; it is through this craving that some have wandered away from the faith and pierced their hearts with many pangs " (I Tim. 6:10).

"Faith Without Works Is Dead"

James is an activist who is probably struggling against a school of thought that drew on slogans of Paul but did not live the life in Christ that Paul knew. These people had understood the apostle to say that faith and works cannot be combined in the Christian faith. Had not Paul said, " For we hold that a man is justified by faith apart from works of law " (Rom. 3:28)? And, " To one who does not work but trusts him who justifies the ungodly, his faith is reckoned as righteousness " (Rom. 4:5)? They seemed to hear Paul say that he who has faith need not work at all, and that he who works shows a lack of faith. Paul, however, was not addressing the issue of activity versus passivity. He was speaking about the source of our reconciliation with God. Against this misunderstood Paulinism the author reacts with the serious phrase, " The hearer must be doer as well " (James 1:22; 2:14-26). Paul himself would never have denied this, since faith for Paul is active in love (Gal. 5:6). So James may not be openly opposed to Paul himself but to a group that claims to be Pauline.

Yet the method by which the author defends his position in James 2:14-26 makes him definitely seem to be against Paul. His argument reveals him as a serious moralist who has not grasped what Paul means by faith and righteousness. Like most of us, he lives by the Jewish-Christian principle of faith *and* works, a principle that was the very denial of the gospel for Paul. There was for Paul a strict either-or: " Did you receive the Spirit by works of the law, or by hearing with faith? " (Gal. 3:2.) " You are severed from Christ, you who would be justified by the law; you have fallen away from grace." (Ch. 5:4.) James understood faith to mean belief in a statement of truth, that is, belief in monotheism (James 2:19). Because of this shallow understanding he arrived at a position opposite to that of Paul. It holds that man is saved by a combination of faith and works. "You see that faith was active along with his works, and faith was perfected by works." (V. 22.)

How does James arrive at his faith-and-works position? Let us trace his argument in ch. 2:14-26. An opponent is introduced (v. 18) who says something like, "Faith is as good as works." James disputes the religious equality of faith and works. (V. 18b.) A confession of monotheism is of no avail in the Last Judgment if it is not accompanied by good deeds. James proceeds to prove his position by an appeal to Scripture. The father of the Jews, Abraham, and the Gentile woman, Rahab, are his material. Abraham, according to Jewish tradition, had to undergo ten tests of faith. The last and greatest of them was the sacrifice of the promise, his only son, Isaac. (Gen., ch. 22.) This act of obedience was the highest proof of his piety. On the basis of this act he was justified before God. (James 2:23.) Similarly, Rahab (Josh. 6:25) receives righteousness as a reward for her good deed (James 2:25).

To what extent and on what point do Paul and James disagree? The point of disagreement revolves around the issue: How can I be acceptable to God? Or, in Biblical terms: How am I justified? The extent to which Paul and James disagree is indicated by the fact that both use the same verse from Scripture (Gen. 15:6) for their Biblical authority: "[Abraham] believed the Lord; and he reckoned it to him as righteousness." But they arrive at opposite conclusions. (Compare Rom. 4:3 with James 2:23.) In Jewish fashion, James underlines the sacrifice of Isaac as Abraham's supreme deed of faith. On the basis of Gen., ch. 22, he interprets Gen. 15:6 to mean that Abraham's faith was his pious act. Paul, on the other hand, stressed Gen. 15:6 as *prior to* the deed of Gen., ch. 22. And Gen. 15:6 means to him that God's "reckoning" justifies Abraham. What makes Abraham acceptable before God is his faith that God has accepted him as he is. This acceptance now is the power that motivates his life and actions.

As one commentator expresses it: " In Judaism, Abraham's faith was reckoned to him as a work of righteousness; in James, his faith and his works were reckoned to him for righteousness; in Paul, this faith was reckoned to him instead of works for righteousness." What James may not have understood was the problem with which Paul wrestled and which shaped his theological thinking. Martin Luther put it clearly: " Good works do not make a good man, but a good man does good works." The trouble with James's opponents was that they would only have understood the first half of Luther's statement. Perhaps James himself would have understood only the second half of it.

James, then, stands in the Jewish-Christian tradition, where the Pauline issue of faith and works was never understood. But in the face of followers of Paul, who perverted Paul, declaring the ethical life to be unimportant, we must appreciate the seriousness of this Christian teacher who gives pilgrims on the way to their heavenly home a manual for their way through this world.

CHAPTER 4 | *The Danger of Backsliding*

As soon as the church attempted to formulate its convictions and became aware of its self-identity in history, counter-movements developed in its own fold. These counter-movements did not manifest themselves suddenly and full-grown, but they were coming into being as gradually and hesitantly as the formulations of the church. It is very difficult to distinguish heresy from orthodoxy in the beginning because no fixed forms and norms existed. What in retrospect we now call orthodoxy might well have been heresy in any particular church in the first and second century. The interpretation of the Christian faith as held by a minority of believers, which we know through their own documents, might well have been considered heretical by the majority of believers whose interpretations are no longer accessible to us. The opponents of James, for instance, might have been real Paulinists, whose views were caricatured by James. We simply do not know, but it makes us wary of hasty conclusions as to what orthodoxy and heresy mean. Identifications will be difficult to make. To single out stages of a process that is complex will inevitably lead to exaggerations. Nevertheless, it appears that heresy takes essentially two forms in this era — a conservative and a radical one.

The conservative pattern. The conservative pattern we call the Judaizing movement, a movement with which Paul had a severe struggle in his churches. These were the Christians who did not understand the radical break with Judaism that the event of Christ introduced. The Jewish-Christian wing of the Church, of which The Letter of James is representative, confessed Christ but tried to seek a compromise with the religion out of which it came.

A second motif may also have been at work here. For connection with Judaism brought with it certain political advantages. In many instances Roman citizenship had been granted to Jews. This meant legal protection against the caprice of provincial officers. Jewish religious societies centering around the synagogues, headed by their own officers, were recognized both as religious and political bodies. Moreover, Jewish monotheism was respected, and the Jew was freed from sharing in the duties of the imperial cults, which would have been inconsistent with his monotheism. Even Jewish religious peculiarities were respected. Some Jews were not required to appear in a court of justice on the Sabbath and were at times excused from military service on that day. Since Judaism was officially a " legitimate religion " in the Roman Empire, a Christianity alienated from Judaism forfeited those privileges. It was suspect and exposed to possible persecution by the Roman government. Paul may have referred to this when, in his struggle with Judaizing tendencies in Galatia, he denounced the Judaizers: " It is those who want to make a good showing in the flesh that would compel you to be circumcised, and only in order that they may not be persecuted for the cross of Christ " (Gal. 6:12).

The radical pattern. The other form of heresy, the radical pattern, expressed itself in terms of Roman-Hellenistic philosophy and religion, a movement closely aligned to Gnosticism. Gnosticism, as we shall see in the next section, expressed a mystical religion in which the salvation of the individual soul came about through knowledge (Greek, *gnosis*). It was a form of religion that resembled certain pseudo-psychological and theosophic movements, which promise salvation of the self through mystic knowledge. It centered around the conviction that man is a stranger on earth and will only come to himself when he despises his body and recovers his divine inner self. But before we enter upon a discussion of this type of heresy, we shall first deal with a document that is concerned with the conservative Judaizing heresy — The Letter to the Hebrews.

The Letter to the Hebrews

This writing is significant because it shows what a variety of theological thought constituted the main stream of Christianity in the first century. We are in the habit of thinking that Paul was virtually the only apostle to the Gentiles, or at least, with John, the only major theologian of the early Christian movement. Thus we regard the Pauline letters as the core of the missionary drive into the world. However, The Letter to the Hebrews reminds us how rich and varied the stream of early Christian thought was. Even the New Testament itself is not the total expression of the life and thought of the early church. It is only a collection of fragments that have been preserved. If this fragmentary collection points to the theological creativity of the early church, how much more must have been present in the rest of the church's life and thought of which we do not know.

The Letter to the Hebrews is one of the most significant, yet one of the most difficult, writings in the New Testament. The average reader may be impressed with certain passages, such as the roll call of faith in ch. 11, but the unity of the book often escapes him because of the intricate theological arguments and the obscure terminology of the author. The main figure of the letter is the ancient king-priest, Melchizedek, who is declared to be " without father or mother or genealogy " (ch. 7:3), and this phrase applies to the letter as well. The Letter to the Hebrews is silent about its author and about the community to which it is addressed. Indeed, we do not even know whether it is a letter, a theological treatise, or a sermon. Furthermore, the movement of thought is unique in the New Testament, since no other writing concentrates so heavily on the cultic and priestly elements of the Christian movement. It is therefore not easy to assign it a historical setting in the apostolic period. What is clear is that the letter was not written by Paul (this was thought even in ancient times), and that it is not addressed to Hebrews, that is, Jews of Palestine. To be sure, the King James Version titles it " The Epistle of Paul the Apostle to the Hebrews," but the earliest manuscripts we possess have simply " To Hebrews." This title itself is not original but was probably added by a second generation, which was impressed by its Hebrew features.

In contrast to the straightforward, practical man, James, we meet in Hebrews a learned theologian, a man who has reflected upon the theological implications of God's act in Christ. Yet he did not reserve his theological reflections for his study but applied them to the concrete situation of his audience. A theological sermon, we might call it. Who then constituted the audience? It was a group of Christians who, in all probability, formed a part of the church at Rome. In ch. 13:24 the author states that " those who come from Italy send you greetings." We know that the church at Rome was divided into several branches, which had grown out of the several synagogues in that city. Thus the church had a mixed character of both Gentile and Jewish-Christian stock.

The author addressed this latter group with a " word of ex-

hortation " (ch. 13:22). Why? Because this Jewish-Christian
wing in the church concentrated too much on its Jewish past,
clung to it for sentimental, theological, or political reasons.
It stuck to the old forms of religion and assimilated its Christian understanding to the old Jewish ways of grace, because
it did not dare to draw the radical implications of Christ's
work for its way of life. This path was the easier because a
link with Judaism may have been beneficial. As we have seen
before, Judaism had been granted a privileged status by the
Roman government, and to surrender this cover of protection
was difficult for the Jewish-Christian branch. Exposure as a
separate religious movement might mean persecution by the
Roman government. Moreover, this wing of the church may
also have been increasingly offended by the crucified Messiah,
by the suffering of the earthly Jesus, since the Messiah was expected to be a glorious figure. Instead of reigning with the
glorified Messiah over their former enemies, they now had to
suffer. (Chs. 10:32; 12:3-4.) And the *Parousia,* which would
vindicate their cause and turn their distress into joy, was not
forthcoming.

APPEAL AND COMFORT

The author preaches to this kind of audience. Indeed, he
intends to *preach.* A " word of exhortation " (ch. 13:22) is his
aim, not theoretical speculation. Awareness of this is essential
for understanding Hebrews. The moral exhortations of the
letter are the primary goal, while the theological sections, interpretations of the Old Testament, and so forth, serve mainly
to underline the exhortations. To this end the author addresses
his preaching. Here was a Christian community that sought
cover under the established ways and institutions of religion.
It had become tired of being a peculiar people among the nations, a " third race " as a later author was to call the Chris-

tians, and it wanted to settle down comfortably in the conditions of this world. Against such a backsliding community the author preaches: "Lift your drooping hands and strengthen your weak knees, and make straight paths for your feet, so that what is lame may not be put out of joint but rather be healed" (ch. 12:12).

With this Jewish-Christian group in mind the author appeals to the fundamental religious truth of the Old Testament and interprets it in the new conditions that God has initiated through the sending of his Son. A basic perspective of the Old Testament was Israel's destiny and mission in history to be a people living solely out of God's hand. Israel should have no visible image of its God and no other support than faith, reliance on God's plan of salvation, and his love. Israel was called to be a pilgrim people, marching through history on nothing but the promise of God. This promise had to be everything to the people or they would have nothing.

"For you are a people holy to the Lord your God; the Lord your God has chosen you to be a people for his own possession, out of all the peoples that are on the face of the earth. It was not because you were more in number than any other people that the Lord set his love upon you and chose you, for you were the fewest of all peoples; but it is because the Lord loves you, and is keeping the oath which he swore to your fathers, that the Lord has brought you out with a mighty hand, and redeemed you from the house of bondage, from the hand of Pharaoh king of Egypt." (Deut. 7:6-8.)

To this pilgrimage, to this hope, and to this faith the author appeals. In this sense his sermon is a "word of exhortation."

The Greek word for exhortation means both comfort and appeal. The people of God are only God's people when they are on the march. As soon as they stand still or fall back or want to "make a deal" with the world, they stand condemned. They will be sentenced with a world over which the hour of judgment is falling. The "appeal" is that they must either march on or succumb. The "comfort" is the reason and foundation for the appeal. It rests in what Christ, the great high priest, has accomplished.

This theological reasoning has determined the literary division of the sermon. Almost throughout the book the exhortations follow upon the theological discussions because the exhortations are based upon them. For example, the first part of the sermon (Heb. 1:1 to 6:20), which introduces the main theological theme (chs. 7:1 to 10:18), is structured as follows:

Part I: Introduction to theme.

1. The Son superior over the angels　　　　　ch. 1
2. Exhortation　　　　　　　　　　　　ch. 2:1-8b
3. Humiliation of the faithful high priest　vs. 8c-18
4. Exhortation　　　　　　　　　　　　ch. 3:1
5. Jesus as Son superior over Moses　　　　vs. 2-6
6. Exhortation　　　　　　　　chs. 3:7 to 4:13
7. Marks of the true high priest　chs. 4:14 to 5:10
8. Exhortation (toward the "solid food")
   or: preface to main theme　　chs. 5:11 to 6:20

One more characteristic of the letter should be noted. The theological foundation of the theme is developed gradually, because the author himself is aware that his theological argument is no simple matter. "About this we have much to say which is hard to explain" (ch. 5:11), he states, referring to Christ as "high priest for ever after the order of Melchizedek." Indeed, it is so hard that he inserts another chapter before he starts to develop his theme. (Ch. 7.)

THE NEW EXODUS

What is the reasoning behind the wandering motif of The Letter to the Hebrews? Why do the people of God have to march through history with nothing but the promise of God? Why this constant appeal to " walking the way," which may mean concretely a walking in suffering? It occurs because the people of God are constituted by a new exodus, the exodus opened up not by the Red Sea but by the blood of Christ, who as the true high priest offered himself as sacrifice. " But when Christ appeared as a high priest of the good things that have come, . . . he entered once for all into the Holy Place, taking not the blood of goats and calves but his own blood, thus securing an eternal redemption." (Ch. 9:11-12.) Without this new exodus there would be no new people of God. For Israel the exodus opened the way to the Promised Land through the desert. So the new exodus leads through the desert of this world to the heavenly world that God will bring about in the near future.

From the beginning the author has this exodus motif in mind. Quoting Ps. 95, he warns the Christians as the new people of God not to follow the example of the people of the first exodus.

> " Today, when you hear his voice,
> do not harden your hearts as in the rebellion,
> on the day of testing in the wilderness. . . .
> I swore in my wrath,
> ' They shall never enter my rest.' "

(Heb. 3:7-8, 11.)

Israel was unable to enter the Promised Land because of unbelief. (Chs. 3:12; 4:2.) For the new people of God, however, there remains " the promise of entering his rest " (ch. 4:1), a promise valid only for those who stake their all on the God of the promise and dare to walk with him alone. " Let us therefore strive to enter that rest, that no one fall by the same sort of disobedience. For the word of God is living and active, sharper than any two-edged sword." (Vs. 11-12.)

In contrast to the desert generation, the Old Testament offers examples of people who did believe (ch. 11). To the author belief means obedience. Obedience is being on the march to the heavenly city to which the promise of God calls. All the people of ch. 11 are in fact displaced persons, refugees from this world on their way to God's world. The author provides small but significant touches to indicate the importance of the wandering motif. Jacob (v. 21) blesses and worships, while " bowing in worship over the head of his staff," the sign of the wanderer of God. In the light of this same motif Abraham is seen as the father of the Christians: " By faith Abraham obeyed when he was called to go out to a place which he was to receive as an inheritance; and he went out, not knowing where he was to go. By faith he sojourned in the land of promise, as in a foreign land, living in tents. . . . For he looked forward to the city which has foundations, whose builder and maker is God " (vs. 8-10).

The situation of the new people of God is similar: " For here we have no lasting city, but we seek the city which is to come " (ch. 13:14). This is similar, but not identical, because the constitution of the new people of God is different. They seek the city that is to come. They are en route to the heavenly Jerusalem (ch. 12:22) only because Christ has opened the way. It is a " [going] forth to him outside the camp," since " [he has] suffered outside the gate in order to consecrate the people through his own blood." (Ch. 13:12-13.) There would be no marching, no hope, no new exodus, no people of God, without Jesus as " forerunner " (ch. 6:20), as the " pioneer " of our salvation (ch. 2:10). Because he has gone before, we can follow. Because he has cut out the way that leads to heaven, we have open access to God. (Ch. 10:22.) The idea of Christ, the high priest, is set in this context.

CHRIST, THE HIGH PRIEST

It is interesting to see how the author develops this main theme. His aim is essentially an elaboration of the liturgical confession of the church. At important moments the confession is introduced as the foundation of the author's meditation:

" Therefore, holy brethren, who share in a heavenly call, consider Jesus, the apostle and high priest of *our confession*." (Ch. 3:1.)

" Since then we have a great high priest who has passed through the heavens, Jesus, the Son of God, let us hold fast *our confession*." (Ch. 4:14.)

" Therefore, brethren, since we have confidence to enter the sanctuary by the blood of Jesus, by the new and living way which he opened for us through the curtain, that is, through his flesh, and since we have a great priest over the house of God, let us draw near with a true heart in full assurance of faith, with our hearts sprinkled clean from an evil conscience and our bodies washed with pure water. Let us hold fast *the confession of our hope* without wavering, for he who promised is faithful." (Ch. 10:19-23.)

The confession of the church is taken from the oath of allegiance that believers took when they entered the church. It is therefore the baptismal confession of faith, as is suggested by the last passage with its reference to sprinkling and washing. The baptismal pledge is allegiance to the risen and exalted Christ. For his exaltation means a break through the curtain of

death to the heavenly home of the Father. " Since therefore the
children share in flesh and blood, he himself likewise partook
of the same nature, that through death he might destroy him
who has the power of death, that is, the devil, and deliver all
those who through fear of death were subject to lifelong bondage." (Ch. 2:14-15.) On this common church confession the
author builds his theological meditation on the Christ, who
through his death and exaltation has been enthroned as Son
of God. We can still discern how the author develops his
theme, for step by step the high priest motif is introduced until it flowers forth in chs. 7 to 10. Lest we get lost in the sac-
rificial terminology and argumentation of the author, let us
distinguish at this point between the method and the purpose
of the meditation on Christ, the high priest.

The method. As we have seen, the author elaborates on the
church's confession. He does this by way of a special interpretation of certain crucial Old Testament passages, especially
Ps. 2; 95; and 110. The interpretation was developed par-
ticularly at Alexandria in Egypt, where our theologian probably wrote. It viewed persons and events of the Old Testament
as shadows that prophesy a future reality. The early church
regarded the Old Testament as a book of predictive prophecy
that in every instance pointed to him in whom the Old Testament was fulfilled, the Christ. Thus the law was seen as " a
shadow of the good things to come " (Heb. 10:1). The Old
Testament place of worship, the tent or tabernacle in the desert, was viewed as a copy and shadow of the heavenly sanctuary (ch. 8:5). And the Old Testament sacrifices pointed to the
unique, eternal sacrifice of Christ (ch. 9:13-14, 26).

The author reflected on two important psalms that the
early church interpreted as Messianic prophecies, Ps. 2 and
110. In Ps. 110:1 he read about the king: " The Lord says to
my Lord: ' Sit at my right hand, till I make your enemies

your footstool.'" In v. 4: "The Lord has sworn and will not change his mind, You are a priest for ever after the order of Melchizedek." He interpreted both verses as prophecies of Christ and combined v. 1 (the Lordship of the risen Christ) with v. 4 (the priesthood of Melchizedek). In Ps. 2:7 he saw, with the early church, a prophecy of Christ's resurrection: "I will tell of the decree of the Lord: He said to me, 'You are my son, today I have begotten you.'"

He now united the functions of Christ as the Son and risen Lord with those of Christ the high priest. Melchizedek, the obscure Old Testament figure of Gen., ch. 14, and Ps. 110, is subjected to typical rabbinic interpretation. This priest who met Abraham, blessed him, and to whom Abraham gave tithes of all his spoils, is the shadow of Christ. In what sense? In the first place he is an eternal priest, like Christ, "without father or mother or genealogy, and has neither beginning of days nor end of life, but resembling the Son of God he continues a priest for ever" (Heb. 7:3). In the second place Melchizedek was superior to the Old Testament Levitical priesthood, because Abraham gave tithes to Melchizedek. This shows two things: (*a*) Abraham is inferior to Melchizedek; and (*b*) the Levitical priesthood, which descended from Abraham (Levi was "in the loins of his ancestor" when Melchizedek met Abraham), is also inferior to Melchizedek, that is, to Christ.

The purpose. This method now serves a twofold theological purpose: First, the theme of the priesthood of Christ makes it possible to show what his resurrection and exaltation really mean. Secondly, it allows the author to show to a backsliding people wanting to settle into the safe realities of their old Jewish religion that the priestly functions of the old and new order are incompatible. The perfect sacrifice of Christ has put an end to all the former insufficient sacrifices. Besides, in God's intention they served merely to point to the future sacrifice of Christ. The introduction of the complex interpretation of Abraham's inferiority to Melchizedek and the constant comparison of the rites of the Old Covenant with those of the New serves an explicit purpose: it shows the impossibility of adhering to a religious system that has no ultimate reality.

Now let us return to the first point. Cross and resurrection are inseparable in early Christian thought. Without the resurrection the cross would be the death of a tragic hero. Without the cross the resurrection would be a miracle, perhaps, but it would not concern us. Cross and resurrection as inseparable entities testify to the fact that God has sent his Son into the world *for us*. His identification with our condition came to a climax in his death for us. And that his death for us means new life is the joy of his resurrection and exaltation. The resurrection is evidence of God's acceptance of Christ's death as a victory over sin. Our author then expresses this unity of the cross and resurrection in his own terms. He sees it foreshadowed in the Old Testament. For that reason he has combined vs. 1 and 4 of Ps. 110, or the Lordship of the risen Christ and his priesthood " for ever after the order of Melchizedek."

For those who were lost and in bondage to the conditions of this world, Christ has opened the way to the Father. This exaltation, the enthronement of the Son in heaven, signifies God's acceptance of his sacrifice. But the glory of Christ's exaltation lies in the obedience of the man Jesus. In this emphasis the author is at one with the author of John's Gospel, who also sees the real meaning of the resurrection in the incarnation and cross. In John, at the moment of deepest darkness, the moment when Jesus' obedience undergoes its greatest test just before the crucifixion, Jesus proclaims, " Now is the Son of man glorified " (John 13:31; see also ch. 12:23). Also in Hebrews the glory of the exaltation receives its deepest meaning in the obedience of the human high priest. " Therefore he had to be made like his brethren in every respect, so that he might become a merciful and faithful high priest in the service of God, to make expiation for the sins of the people. For because he himself has suffered and been tempted, he is able to help those who are tempted." (Heb. 2:17-18.)

No one in the New Testament, not even in the Synoptic Gospels, portrays so vividly the depth of the human life of Christ as high priest with its pitfalls and temptations. " In the days of his flesh, Jesus offered up prayers and supplications, with loud cries and tears, to him who was able to save him from death, and he was heard for his godly fear. Although he was a Son, he learned obedience through what he suffered; and being made perfect he became the source of eternal salvation to all who obey him, being designated by God a high priest after the order of Melchizedek." (Ch. 5:7-10.) The obedience of the high priest is crucial for the constitution of the people of God, because it is an obedience not enacted for the high priest himself but " on our behalf." This is the meaning of the high priest Christ, whose sacrifice is " not the blood of goats and calves but his own blood, thus securing an eternal redemption " (ch. 9:12). And to indicate the lasting significance of the sacrifice of Christ once for all on Golgotha, the author stresses the eternal priesthood of Christ, " priest for ever after the order of Melchizedek." For now, " seated at the right hand of the throne of the Majesty in heaven " (ch. 8:1), he intercedes permanently for the people of God, " since he always lives to make intercession for them " (ch. 7:25). Therefore, the way of the people of God through the desert of this world, which is a way of suffering, is nevertheless a joyful way, for they walk as sons following the Son (cf. ch. 2:10).

Through suffering to glory — that is the pattern of the Christian pilgrimage.

This is why the preacher's word of exhortation is both appeal and comfort. It is *appeal,* for we have to follow the Son, who learned obedience through what he suffered. Therefore, we must " go forth to him outside the camp, bearing abuse for him " (ch. 13:13), and like Moses we must consider " abuse suffered for the Christ greater wealth than the treasures of Egypt " (ch. 11:26). But this appeal is joyful *comfort* as well, for Christ has gone before, so that we may have hope. " We have this as a sure and steadfast anchor of the soul, a hope that enters into the inner shrine behind the curtain, where Jesus has gone as a forerunner on our behalf." (Ch. 6:19-20.) " On our behalf," the author says. That is the joy of our pilgrimage. For the high priest who has entered the heavens intercedes for the pilgrims: " Consequently he is able for all time to save those who draw near to God through him, since he always lives to make intercession for them " (ch. 7:25).

Such is the situation of the Christian pilgrim: lonely and abused in the world, without any securities or safeguards except the word of God, the word of promise, yet secretly surrounded by a " great . . . cloud of witnesses " who watch intently. The author uses the image of a marathon race held in a stadium that is packed with spectators. And the race can be won only by those who fix their gaze on Him who for their sake has gone before, on him who is the true high priest and forerunner. We run, " looking to Jesus the pioneer and perfecter of our faith, who for the joy that was set before him endured the cross, despising the shame, and is seated at the right hand of the throne of God " (ch. 12:2).

This is the climax of the sermon. The author used all the methods of Old Testament interpretation to point the way for the people of God. Addressing himself to the danger of a retreat into Judaism, the author pointed out that looking back meant falling back into a means of grace that had ended. Moving forward is the only way. And that way is the way of the cross, the way of Him who in his cross and resurrection is "the way, and the truth, and the life."

CHAPTER 5 | *The Threat of Heresy*

T HE danger of heresy was characteristic of this era as a whole. We have already noticed that we cannot understand the Pastoral Epistles unless we see them in the setting of the threat of heresy. In The Letter to the Hebrews we found a conservative heresy: the retreat to Judaism. We shall now deal with the opposite form of heresy: the radical pattern. We must not think that this heresy is dealt with only in the five writings of the New Testament with which we are here concerned. Yet I, II, and III John, II Peter, and Jude form a certain unity because they all deal with that form of heresy which eventually constituted one of the most severe threats to the church: *Gnosticism*. We meet it in its initial stages in the literature we are dealing with. But in the second century it developed into such a formidable movement that it nearly suffocated the church. The great heretics of the second century (Marcion, Apelles, Basilides, and Valentinus) built their systems on the foundations of this early form of Gnosticism. We can perceive the heat of the struggle in the works of the church fathers. Irenaeus (about A.D. 180), for example, wrote five books in which he passionately refuted their beliefs.

BACKGROUND OF GNOSTICISM

Gnosticism did not arise in a vacuum. It first appeared as a climate of thought in the Roman Empire. It was indistinct, yet it was " in the air "; it pervaded the culture and found expression in a variety of ways. It had close connections with other religious movements in the Roman Empire. A mixture of religious elements were blended when different nations and their religions became absorbed in the conglomeration of peoples that constituted the Roman Empire. Because of this melting pot of ideas, it is a complex matter to trace and delineate the various elements that made up Gnosticism.

Fundamental ties existed between this movement and the mystery religions. These religions consisted of worshiping various gods and goddesses of original national significance. They shared a common pattern. All promised their believers salvation by an escape from this evil world of death to the immortal realm of the gods. The worship service of the mystery religions enacted the drama of the cult hero, the redeemer god. The drama told the story of the life of the cult hero and climaxed in his death and rising again. Sacraments let the worshiper participate in the drama of the god and promised him immortal life. The mystery of nature has always had profound influences on man's religious expectations. Basically the cult hero of the mystery religions represented nature's yearly cycle of dying (winter) and rising (spring). Gnosticism, then, was indebted partly to the mystery religions, but it also owed much to certain philosophical and psychological ideas, derived mainly from the philosophy of Plato with its opposition between (heavenly) form and (earthly) matter.

What is Gnosticism? The term is derived from the Greek word *gnosis* (knowledge), and it refers to a spirituality in which a mystic, intuitive knowledge is seen as the way to salvation. This knowledge is not of man's own doing but is regarded as revealed to man by God. It is supposed to reveal to man the truth about creation and about himself. The Gnostic was a profound pessimist, convinced that the Creation was a fatal mistake. Heaven and earth, spirit and matter, simply did not meet. The earth itself existed only because of a great tragedy that at one time shook the divine harmony of the heavens. This absolute split between spirit and matter we call dualism. Salvation for the Gnostic consisted, basically, in overcoming this dualism by denying the reality of matter. The way of salvation was the way from this evil, material earth, through the heavenly regions, back to the pure spirit of the father, the ground of all being.

This kind of religiosity expresses a drive that is inherent in modern forms of mysticism and theosophy. In fact, it connects with a basic psychological problem of the human personality. Gnostic man feels different and alienated from his environment. He feels that the transitoriness of existence and the suffering and decay of earthly life are essentially hostile to his very being. For he believes that he is godlike in his innermost being and he craves immortality. The classic quest to which Gnosticism gives an answer is: Who were we? What have we become? Into what have we been cast? To what goal are we hastening? How shall we be redeemed?

In other words, the Gnostic drama is a projection of man's self-understanding. Gnosticism narrates, basically, the story of the self's tragic fall. Its home is in heaven. It has fallen into this evil world and is now caught in it, and its only hope is to escape from this present darkness to its heavenly home. Thus Gnosticism gives us a glance into the feelings of some people in the Roman Empire. Their experience of life showed that not everything was peace in the *Pax Romana*, the Roman era of peace. Man felt unrooted and estranged under the domination of evil powers, which ruled him and to which he had no resistance.

Gnosticism and the Gospel. When this pagan Gnostic consciousness came into contact with the Christian gospel, it saw enough likeness to adapt itself to it. Had not Paul proclaimed the descent of a Redeemer, who redeemed man from the evil world to the world of God? Was not Christ's incarnation the manifestation of a new God who annulled the law and the creation of the God of the Jews? In this era, when Gnosticism was still in its initial stages, the battle lines were not clearly drawn. Gnostic teachers invaded the church in Asia Minor and attracted house churches to their way of thinking. The lines of division between orthodoxy and heresy gradually became more marked.

Later, opposition to the dualism of the Gnostics increased. The orthodox leaders argued that if matter were evil and had no connection with God, the God of creation was denied. Then the body was evil as well. God's sovereignty over his creation and his purpose in history were at stake. Two consequences would follow: (*a*) the humanity of Jesus could not be the incarnation of God; and (*b*) the Word had not become flesh but only seemingly so. Indeed, Gnosticism did not really hold to the incarnation at all. To say that Jesus was God incarnate is to say that God became flesh. But if flesh is necessarily evil and has no connection at all with God, the Gnostics had to say that Christ only " seemed " to be flesh. (This heresy is called *Docetism,* from the Greek verb, *dokein,* " to seem.") Furthermore, how man treats his own body and relates to other " bodies " is irrelevant. Such spiritualism, such dualism of soul and body, left no place for interest in one's neighbor. And so love for the neighbor and concern for one's brother in the church were perverted into a spiritual egotism.

We can readily understand the profound issues at stake here: if God and matter are declared to be hostile to each other, then creation is meaningless; life in the body becomes something to be feared and hated; and life and action in the world are doomed to fail. In a scheme where God has lost control of creation, creation becomes the seat of demonic evil, which frustrates all moral virtue and action. People start talking about "the meaninglessness of existence."

It is against the Gnostic setting that we must understand the five writings under consideration: the three letters of John, II Peter, and Jude. They probably all originated in Asia Minor, where in the first century the threat of the Gnostic heresy arose.

HERESY AND ORTHODOXY (II and III JOHN)

We must see I John against the background of II and III John if we want to keep close to the historical situation in which these epistles arose. II and III John are letters in the strict sense. II John is directed to a specific community and III John to a person in a community. I John, on the other hand, is truly a catholic epistle, a pastoral letter from "the elder," a district supervisor over house churches, intended for the whole circuit of his churches. II and III John were intended for specific churches that may have belonged to the same circuit.

II and III John picture the atmosphere of a time pervaded by controversy. We can see that the situation between "orthodoxy" and "heresy" was very fluid. In III John a church head, Diotrephes, does not want to subject himself to the elder or supervisor and therefore bans his emissaries. Because of this, Diotrephes is condemned as an evil man who "has not seen God" (III John 11). Possibly Diotrephes heads a majority in a church that dislikes the inroads the elder and his emissaries want to make. Diotrephes on his part may consider the elder a heretic! In II John we see the elder practicing the same techniques for which he calls Diotrephes an atheist: "If anyone comes to you and does not bring this doctrine, do not receive him into the house or give him any greeting; for he who greets him shares his wicked work." (V. 10.) How interesting it would be if we could have access to the views of the other side! How would Diotrephes have spoken about the elder? At any rate, this state of affairs must caution us not to accept all accusations at face value. For example, the author of I John says of the heretics, " They went out from us, but they were not of us; for if they had been of us, they would have continued with us." (Ch. 2:19.) We do not, of course, hear the opinion of those who have withdrawn. But the author wants to make a theological point: " They are of the world, therefore what they say is of the world, and the world listens to them " (ch. 4:5). Since true Christians are " of God " (v. 4), the heretics cannot belong to them. However, the repeated warnings in I John and in III John 9 and 10, show that the situation within the churches was more complex than the author cared to indicate.

Religious propaganda can be quite vicious, as we shall see when we consider the method and language of debate. But in the midst of this debate, an important issue is at stake: " the coming of Jesus Christ in the flesh " (II John 7). It is this " doctrine " (v. 9) that decides whether the church will be the church of Jesus Christ or some sort of religious society. I John will explicate what is at stake here.

HERESY AND CHRISTOLOGY (I JOHN)

This letter is one of the great pieces of literature in the New Testament. Its author was probably a superintendent over a church area in Asia Minor. He may have been the author of the Fourth Gospel, so similar to it are his language, style, and thought. The letter combines a profound meditation on the nature of the Christian faith with a severe attack upon the heretical dangers of the time. The author embroiders upon a simple pattern. His circular argumentation sets the meditative mood of the epistle. Again and again the same ideas occur: God is light, love, and truth. To be a child of God is to be of the truth and to walk in the light, which means to love one's brother. To hate one's brother is to walk in darkness, for one cannot love God and hate one's brother. And these ideas circle around the central conviction of the incarnation: " In this is love, not that we loved God but that he loved us and sent his Son to be the expiation for our sins. Beloved, if God so loved us, we also ought to love one another " (I John 4:10-11).

This seemingly calm meditation was written in the midst of a severe crisis, and it contains a bitter attack against enemies of the church. The world was attempting to disintegrate the church, and the champions of the world were the heretics. " Children, it is the last hour; and as you have heard that antichrist is coming, so now many antichrists have come; therefore we know that it is the last hour." (Ch. 2:18.) There could be no compromise between the church and its opponents. It was a case of black and white to John. He therefore did not hesitate to call his opponents " children of the devil " (ch. 3:10) and murderers (v. 15). John described the conflict in terms of the ultimate crisis of history. The early Christians believed that prior to the glorious Return of Christ there would be a period of sharp distress, temptation, and persecution. The Johannine Christ had expressed it this way: " When a woman is in travail she has sorrow, because her hour has come; but when she is delivered of the child, she no longer remembers the anguish for joy that a child is born into the world. So you have sorrow now, but I will see you again and your hearts will rejoice, and no one will take your joy from you " (John 16:21-22). Just prior to Christ's Return, " false Christs and false prophets will arise and show signs and wonders, to lead astray, if possible, the elect " (Mark 13:22).

John believed that the situation of his day represented the

ultimate crisis of history. For his opponents' teaching was threatening the very foundation of the church's faith: the confession that " Jesus Christ has come in the flesh " (I John 4:2). This coming in the flesh, Christ's incarnation, was the manifestation of God's love. For by sending his Son into man's condition, God was reconciling man to himself by cleansing him from sin (chs. 1:9; 2:2, 12; 3:5). The church's unity lies in its response to that love. For John, the dividing line between belief and unbelief, between light and darkness, is the confession of the incarnation. Such a confession does not merely point to an emotional feeling of love on God's part. It points rather to the translation of that feeling into action. God's love is not mere sentiment, which reaches the soul and not the body. It is the act of self-giving love, which reaches down to the whole of man, body and soul together. This is the meaning of the incarnation for John.

Therefore, ecstasy of prophets or other utterances ascribed to the Spirit (ch. 4:1-3) mean nothing if they deny the incarnation. For the Spirit is only the Holy Spirit if it is the Spirit of Christ, that is, if it bears witness to the reality of Christ's life, suffering, and resurrection as the sole foundation of Christian faith. (Ch. 4:1-6.) John refers to this when he writes: " That which was from the beginning, which we have heard, which we have seen with our eyes, which we have looked upon and touched with our hands " (ch. 1:1). We are men of history. If salvation means anything at all, it concerns actual and tangible people, living ordinary lives in a society of men. The incarnation affirms that God accepts and redeems us as we actually are, not as we imagine ourselves to be in the depth of our being. " In this is love, not that we loved God but that he loved us and sent his Son to be the expiation for our sins." (Ch. 4:10.)

The heretics, who denied that God could have anything to do with matter, divided Christ into a divine element, which descended upon him at baptism, and a human element. Their dualism forced them to deny any real connection between the Spirit and the body. The human element, Christ's body, was nothing more than clothing for the divine element, and it perished in the way of all flesh. In this way Christ became the symbol and example for the life of every Gnostic. The Gnostic was exceedingly spiritual. But his " spiritual being " was confined to his inner self, for his body was perishable and hostile to God. It hindered the true destiny of his being.

Indeed, all creation was evil and was to be shunned. The consequence of such a faith is preoccupation with the self and rejection of one's neighbor. One is not concerned with the stuff of creation, social or otherwise. Therefore, the denial of the incarnation carried with it a denial of ethics, of love for one's brother. Worse still, the Gnostic described man's condition in terms of a tragic fate. Sin meant the tragedy of man's existence on earth, for which man was not responsible. The Gnostic denied the Christian assertion that sin is the rebellion of the creature against God, and that man is therefore responsible for sin. (Chs. 2:1-2; 3:4-9, 19-24.)

In contrast to this, the main line of attack by John is directed against this denial of ethics. His opponents proudly proclaim: " I am in the light "; " I know him "; " I am spiritually perfect "; " I have no sin "; " I participate in him." Against such slogans the elder retorts: " You are a liar "; " you are in darkness "; and, worse still, " you make God a liar " because you " do not keep his commandments," which means that " you do not love your brother." (See chs. 1:5 to 2:6.) To love one's brother is to maintain the unity of the church, for the unity of the church is the bulwark against divisive heresy. (Ch. 2:19.) To dwell in unity is to " abide in him " (chs. 2:28; 3:24) and to be " of the truth " (chs. 2:21; see also ch. 5:20). To abide in God is to abide in love. " God is love, and he who abides in love abides in God, and God abides in him." (Ch. 4:16.) Only he who abides in God knows the truth and is in the truth: "We are in him who is true, in his Son Jesus Christ" (ch. 5:20). The unity of the church is a unity of truth and love. (Ch. 1:7.) The truth of God's love in Christ (ch. 4:9) makes possible a life in truth, that is, in love of one's brother (ch. 2:4; see also ch. 1:6).

The incarnation of Christ is the foundation of everything else. "No one who denies the Son has the Father. He who confesses the Son has the Father also." (Ch. 2:23.) The absolute definitions of God that John gives are unique in the New Testament: "God is love" (ch. 4:8, 16) and "God is light" (ch. 1:5). They take on concrete meaning in that Jesus Christ's incarnation is the living manifestation and proof of this love and light. (Ch. 4:9.) Because of God's love in Christ, we may call God our Father. We do not call God Father simply because we are his creatures; the title does not come naturally to our lips. To call God Father is a privilege given only to those who have become the "children of God." And these are the ones who abide in Him who "appeared to take away sins" (ch. 3:5).

HERESY AND THE KINGDOM OF GOD (II PETER, JUDE)

Gnostic heresy came into conflict not only with the church's confession of Christ but also with its eschatology — the hope for the Kingdom of God. This refers to the conviction of the Christians that they live in "the last times," the final period of history, which will soon bring to sight what the Christian now holds in faith. The Lordship of God in Christ over all his creation will be made manifest when Christ returns in glory. The conflict over the Christian hope was already apparent in I John, who, as we have seen, was conscious of living in the final period of history. (I John 2:18.)

II Peter is the latest book of the New Testament. It was

written about A.D. 150, probably in Asia Minor, and it reflects the situation of a few decades after I John. The author wrote under the name of the apostle Peter in order to enhance his "apostolic" prestige with the churches receiving his correspondence. The letter is completely devoted to one topic: the problem of the delay of the Kingdom of God. "The Lord is not slow about his promise, as some count slowness, but is forbearing toward you. . . . But the day of the Lord will come like a thief." (Ch. 3:9-10.) II Peter is a defense of Christian eschatology directly mainly against Gnostic teachers. The Gnostics seem to have been quite successful in gathering adherents among the Christian churches, with their denial of the Return of Christ and of any hope for the establishment of the Kingdom of God. The author of II Peter quoted almost the whole letter of Jude in his second chapter. He did so because he agreed with the anti-heretical language of Jude. "For, uttering loud boasts of folly, they entice with licentious passions of the flesh men who have barely escaped from those who live in error." (Ch. 2:18; see Jude 17-21.) He may also have thought that Jude deserved more of a hearing than it had actually received in the churches.

The delay of Christ's Return brought with it skepticism and doubt. This has been a problem for the church ever since the second century. If Christ came to introduce the new era of God's Kingdom, how long must Christians wait for the final resurrection, the coming of the Kingdom? Is the hope for the Return of Christ a great mistake, a misunderstanding of the Christian gospel? The opponents ask: "Where is the promise of his coming? For ever since the fathers fell asleep, all things have continued as they were from the beginning of creation." (II Peter 3:4.) The mockery is apparent in the question. The Gnostics thought they had the answer: the creation would never be the scene of redemption. They taught that redemption must be understood in a spiritualistic sense: that God in Christ had made us free from the world of matter; that the Spirit that God had given us had transformed us; that man carried a divine self within him, and upon the death of the body it would soar again to the heavens.

In other words, the Gnostics spiritualized the hope for the bodily resurrection, which the Christians associated with the Return of Christ. Their conviction was similar to that of the Gnostics quoted in II Tim. 2:18, who held "that the resurrection is past already." The Christian hope is directed to God's Lordship over all his creation. The Gnostics, however, spiritualized this Lordship and located it in man's innermost being. Eschatology and the final resurrection meant to them the denial of creation, not its perfection. It meant the extraction of man's spiritual self from his lower nature, not a completion of the whole man. This spiritualization of the hope went hand in hand with a perfectionism that saw life in the Kingdom as realized in the present. Had not Paul proclaimed himself as a man completely filled with the Spirit? Did he not make a distinction between the "mature" and the "babes in Christ," between those who were "spiritual men" and those who were "men of the flesh" (I Cor. 3:1-2)? The Gnostics thought that they were the mature who could take the "solid food" of Christian teaching, as over against the ordinary Christians, the "babes in Christ."

II Peter's answer. The defense of the coming Kingdom was a formidable task, and unfortunately the author of II Peter did not accomplish it clearly. In the first place we see that abuse replaced debate. A superficial look at both Jude and II Peter gives us the impression that the opponents were the vilest and most lustful creatures on earth. Although this is the impression the authors intended, it should not be accepted as unbiased truth. We encounter here the character of second-century church polemic. The church could not afford a debate, either because of the intellectual shallowness of some of its leaders or because of the dangerous success of Gnostics among church members. This simply necessitated a struggle for survival. The Old Testament prophets had denounced idolatry as adultery. Therefore, sexual perversity was the most natural charge. In this vein the author attacked the heretics: " They count it pleasure to revel in the daytime. They are blots and blemishes, reveling in their dissipation, carousing with you. They have eyes full of adultery, insatiable for sin. They entice unsteady souls " (II Peter 2:13-14). This is something like Jeremiah's oracle: " Surely, as a faithless wife leaves her husband, so have you been faithless to me, O house of Israel, says the Lord." (Jer. 3:20; see also Hos. 1:2.)

In the second place, the author defended himself by an appeal to holy tradition. " Peter " stood in the line of apostolic succession (II Peter 1:1-3). The apostolic line transmitted the sacred history, and the authority of this sacred history was sufficient to overthrow heresy. " Peter " had himself witnessed the Savior, even in his glorification on the mountain (vs. 16-18). The glorification on the mountain was the guarantee of the coming glory of the Kingdom. Indeed, the apostles were endowed with the great promise of the Kingdom of God and the escape from a sinful world (v. 4). They alone could interpret Scripture in the way it was meant to be explained (ch. 1:19; see also ch. 3:16). For they alone had the Spirit. Therefore, the Gnostic teachers had no business propagating their own explanations of Scripture. Only the legitimate ministry might do so. For " no prophecy of scripture is a matter of one's own interpretation." (Ch. 1:20.) The defender of orthodox eschatology was the legitimate interpreter of the sacred truth. We see here the development of the ministry toward that of the early Catholic Church. The legitimate (that is, apostolic) ministry was the basis for Scriptural interpretation, because the Spirit was now primarily channeled through the legitimate ministry.

In the third place, we may have some questions about the defense of eschatology itself. Here the author operated with a double criterion. On the one hand, he appealed to early Christian eschatology, to the belief in the suddenness of the end. (Ch. 3:10; see Mark 13:35; I Thess. 5:2.) But on the other hand, he suspended this expectation by introducing a different notion of time. " With the Lord one day is as a thousand years, and a thousand years as one day." (Ch. 3:8, quoting Ps. 90:4.)

The meaning of eschatology. Even though II Peter did employ an unsatisfactory method, the author was concerned with an issue of the first importance. If with the Gnostics we " spiritualize " eschatology and salvation, that is, separate them from God's created order and from God's history, we have really limited God's sovereignty. We have said, in effect, that the power of evil in the world is too strong for God. Yet it is essential that the church hold fast to its confession that God is the Lord of creation and of history and is not merely the God of man's inner self. The Redeemer of man is also the Creator of the world and the Lord of history. If we surrender that which he has created as something with which he really can do nothing, we are no longer speaking of the God of the Bible, " who has measured the waters in the hollow of his hand and marked off the heavens with a span " (Isa. 40:12), who " looks on the earth and it trembles, who touches the mountains and they smoke " (Ps. 104:32). As the author expressed it: " They [the Gnostics] deliberately ignore this fact, that by the word of God heavens existed long ago, and an earth formed out of water and by means of water " (II Peter 3:5).

Furthermore, if we fail to assert God's sovereignty over creation and history, we have become infected with a misunderstanding of ourselves. The Christian, indeed, sees that God has a purpose that is above and beyond creation and history, but he cannot elevate himself over them in a feeling of his own superiority. For the Christian, like every man, is man, involved in the very stuff of creation. If he denies this, he inevitably imagines himself to be a perfected person, and he transforms God, the Lord of creation, into a means for his own glorification.

The point at issue in early Christian eschatology was the glory and majesty of God and the conviction that man can only live " by faith, not by sight " (II Cor. 5:7). The Christian lives between a redemption that has occurred and a redemption that will occur. To trust in the first and to hope for the second is what the Christian means by faith. For faith does not proclaim its own perfection or the lordship of man, but points a way to him who is the Lord over all of life and by whose grace man is redeemed. Faith, then, is inseparable from hope. " Therefore, brethren, be the more zealous to confirm your call and election, for if you do this you will never fall; so there will be richly provided for you an entrance into the eternal kingdom of our Lord and Savior Jesus Christ." (II Peter 1:10-11.) " But you, beloved, build yourselves up on your most holy faith; pray in the Holy Spirit; keep yourselves in the love of God; wait for the mercy of our Lord Jesus Christ unto eternal life." (Jude 20-21.)

CHAPTER 6 | *The Call to Pilgrimage*

THE church was not only threatened from within. As soon as it was identified as a movement separate from Judaism the church faced the danger of persecution by the state and the insecurity of being a religion without legal status in the Roman Empire. This danger, to which more than one " alien " religion was subject, became actuality for the Christian church through the pressure of public opinion. In I Peter and The Revelation this situation can be most clearly discerned.

For Western Christians, whose society tends to identify Christianity with its own culture, there is reason to reflect on the true meaning of being a Christian. Does it denote basically an accommodation to the " ways of the world," or an antithesis to them? Do we realize sufficiently that the church is the *ekklesia* — the people of God " called out " of their environment to the Kingdom of God? Let us see how the people of God at the turn of the first century reacted to the pressures and persecution of the world around them.

I PETER

I Peter takes us to Asia Minor, probably in the early decades of the second century. The Emperor Trajan (A.D. 98–117) sought to strengthen the eastern borders of the Roman Empire against the " danger from the east," the Parthians. For this purpose he needed two things: (1) unification of the Empire, and (2) good lines of communication with the east, so that the border legions could easily be supplied with manpower. Therefore, he sent a personal appointee, Pliny, to the east to secure tranquillity in the border provinces. These provinces north of the Taurus Mountains, comprising most of present Turkey, were a seedbed of unrest. The masses had been subjected to a bad administration for years, and the provinces, although rich in resources, had systematically been plundered by Rome. As a consequence local uprisings were the order of the day, and all local organizations were suspect. Pliny, then, had to enforce a policy of centralization that religion was required to serve. Homage to the state gods and to the statue of the emperor meant an oath of allegiance to the state.

We can imagine how the bands of Christians, aloof from society and subject to gossip about their " secret meetings," became the objects of suspicion in these security-conscious eastern provinces. In Pliny's correspondence with Trajan we read of Christians' being denounced and persecuted. Pliny asked Trajan for advice on the prosecution proceedings with regard to the Christians. This indicates that thus far legal insecurity for the Christians had not issued in actual prosecution. Indeed, apart from the local persecution at Rome under Nero, Christians were the subject of gossip rather than police action. It was rumored that in secret gatherings they practiced incest, murder, and cannibalism.

Pliny reported to Trajan on his progress:

> " Meanwhile this is what I did in the case of those who were reported to me as Christians. I asked them if they were Christians; if they confessed, I asked them a second and third time while threaten-

ing them with punishment. If they persevered, I ordered them led away [to execution]. I had no doubt that whatever they admitted, certainly their determination and inflexible obstinacy ought to be punished. Then, as usually happens, the progress of the investigation made the accusations more numerous and more cases arose. An anonymous accusation was brought before me with many names in it. Those who denied that they either were or had been Christians, I had invoke the gods of my dictation and worship your statue with incense and wine. . . . Moreover I had them curse Christ, and it is said that those who are really Christians cannot be forced to do any of these things. . . . The contagion of that superstition has penetrated not only the cities but even the villages and the country. But it can probably be checked and corrected."

Around this time I Peter was written. An elder of Asia Minor wrote under the name of the apostle Peter to the districts of Asia Minor — " Pontus, Galatia, Cappadocia, Asia, and Bithynia " (ch. 1:1) — in order to strengthen them for the coming persecution (ch. 4:12), and to point to a way of life that befits Christians in their imminent trials. Some scholars maintain that the letter is much earlier than the time of Trajan and may come from the hand of Peter himself. Whichever date one assigns it, the understanding of I Peter is not seriously affected.

Baptism and pilgrimage. Why is the Christian a " displaced person," an exile in the world? Why is it his " privilege " that he is chosen or " called " to suffer (chs. 1:1; 2:20-21)? Why should the grace of God mean disgrace in the world? This is the theme of I Peter, and it is expressed as an answer to the situation of actual suffering and persecution. The theme of the letter may be outlined as follows:

I. The Greeting: " To the [chosen] exiles of the dispersion "   ch. 1:1-2
II. The Sermon: Walk in hope   chs. 1:3 to 4:11
   A. Doxology: Rebirth to a living hope   ch. 1:3-12
   B. The walk as exiles motivated   chs. 1:13 to 2:10
   C. The walk as exiles in daily life   chs. 2:11 to 3:12
   D. The walk as exiles means suffering   chs. 3:13 to 4:11
III. The Letter: The actuality of suffering for the Christian   chs. 4:12 to 5:11
IV. Conclusion   ch. 5:12-14

As the outline suggests, the author has applied a sermon, given previously at the time of baptism, to the new situation in which the baptized Christians find themselves. His main purpose is to point out that the present situation of the Christians is nothing but a consequence of their baptismal confession and pledge. This accounts for the fact that I Peter seems to fall into two parts: the baptismal sermon and the letter. The baptismal sermon is a catechism, teaching new Gentile converts how to live in the midst of a pagan world (especially chs. 2:11 to 4:11). It reminds new converts of their baptismal instruction and draws from ethical lists used in Christian teaching. The sermon envisions the possibility of public calumny and persecution. (Chs. 1:6-7; 2:20; 3:14.) In the letter (chs. 4:12 to 5:11) that possibility has become an actuality.

Baptism means rebirth to a new way of life, which involves a radical break with the former life. " By his great mercy we have been born anew to a living hope through the resurrection of Jesus Christ from the dead, and to an inheritance . . . for a salvation ready to be revealed in the last time." (Ch. 1:3-5.) Baptism gives a foretaste of salvation in the Kingdom of God, and it points to the realization of that salvation. Therefore, I Peter is often called the epistle of hope. For the " living hope " (ch. 1:3) is, as it were, the nutrition, the milk of the newborn Christians. "Like newborn babes, long for the pure spiritual milk, that by it you may grow up to salvation; for you have tasted the kindness of the Lord." (Ch. 2:2-3.)

So the salvation of the Kingdom of God is the object of the hope, described by the author as " an inheritance . . . kept in heaven " (ch. 1:4). The inheritance was, for Israel, God's promise to Abraham to give the chosen people Palestine as their true home, to which they had to march through the desert. But there would have been no marching if God's mighty arm had not redeemed them from the bondage of Egypt and had not led them through the Red Sea. In the same way the author sees the Christians, the new people of God, on the march to their true home, the Kingdom of God. (Chs. 1:3, 5; 3:15; 4:7; 5:4, 6, 10.) Their inheritance, however, is not of this earth but " imperishable, undefiled, and unfading, kept in heaven " (ch. 1:4). And the Dispersion (v. 1) is not to Egypt or any geographical area, but the spiritual condition of Christians in this world. The Christians are the New Israel for whom life in this world is life in exile, just as for Israel life outside Palestine and Jerusalem was life in exile. " Conduct yourselves with fear throughout the time of your exile." (Ch. 1:17.)

The language of the exodus story pervades the baptismal sermon. In baptism, Christians have been redeemed from the house of bondage, the slavery to the passions and conditions of this world (chs. 1:18; 4:3-4). Their Passover lamb is Christ. His blood has made possible their redemption from bondage.

(Ch. 1:19.) "You know that you were ransomed from the futile ways inherited from your fathers, . . . with the precious blood of Christ, like that of a lamb without blemish or spot." (Ch. 1:18-19; see also chs. 2:24; 3:18.) Therefore, they must now gird their loins, marching to the Promised Land, which is already in sight (ch. 1:13). Baptism conveys to us the death of Christ as a death for our sins. For his death means the death of our past life of sin (ch. 4:3-4), and his resurrection a new birth (ch. 2:2), which implies a new way of life.

Pilgrimage in the world. The author concentrates on the meaning of baptism for daily living. He assumes that his readers understand baptism in order to concentrate on what is the more urgent need: how to walk in the midst of this world, and specifically how to behave amidst slander and persecution. Central in this appeal is the Person of Jesus Christ. The One who has redeemed us from our bondage is the Shepherd and Guardian of our souls. (Chs. 2:25; 5:4.) We shall know him only if and when we know his way. And his way went through suffering to glory in complete obedience to the Father who sent him. So the Christian way is the same way: from suffering to glory (ch. 1:11). In this sense we have been called to suffer, "because Christ also suffered for you, leaving you an example, that you should follow in his steps. He committed no sin; no guile was found on his lips. When he was reviled, he did not revile in return; when he suffered, he did not threaten; but he trusted to him who judges justly" (ch. 2:21-23).

The author's stress on the imitation of Christ is a necessary reminder to every Christian that he cannot grasp the significance of Christ's death or atonement without following in Christ's way of suffering. "If any man would come after me, let him deny himself and take up his cross and follow me." (Mark 8:34.) Only when we take up his way can we begin to understand what his death for us means. And the imitation of Christ is not a sentimental, unrealistic appeal, good for a Sunday meditation but irrelevant to the harsh conditions of the world. " To do right " in I Peter (chs. 2:12, 14-15, 20; 3:17; 4:19) emphasizes the concreteness of the imitation of Christ.

The peculiar attitude of the Christian hope reveals itself here. It is one thing to be a pilgrim, another to be a revolutionary. As long as the present order is permitted by God, one must endure in the midst of it, although one does not belong to it (ch. 5:10). To be " in the world but not of it " is the watchword. So even in the face of persecution " if one suffers as a Christian " (ch. 4:16), one must not rebel. The author counsels moderation in the face of persecution by the state, an attitude sharply different from the vehement attack upon the state as " Babylon . . . mother of harlots " in Rev. 17:5. " Be subject for the Lord's sake to every human institution, whether it be to the emperor as supreme, or to governors." (I Peter 2:13-14.) " For one is approved if, mindful of God, he endures pain while suffering unjustly. . . . For to this you have been called, because Christ also suffered for you." (Ch. 2:19, 21.) " If one suffers as a Christian, let him not be ashamed, but under that name let him glorify God." (Ch. 4:16.)

The present order is the scene of suffering and redeeming love. " Do not return evil for evil or reviling for reviling; but on the contrary bless, for to this you have been called." (Ch. 3:9.) The Christian pilgrim can have this " royal " conduct because of his baptism, which makes the coming of the Kingdom a sure reality by breaking with the past and re-creating Christians as new children in God's grace. Therefore, the author depicts that event as the culmination of all history. God's way of salvation from the very beginning of Old Testament times pointed to this event. Everyone in the Old Testament seemed to point his finger at it, and even the angels in heaven stood on their toes to peep at its marvels (ch. 1:10-12).

The mighty hand of God has in Christ made this new birth possible, and he will bring it to a secure end. Therefore, the Christian pilgrimage is joy and suffering at the same time. Both are the work of the mercy of God: " Humble yourselves therefore under the mighty hand of God, that in due time he may exalt you " (ch. 5:6). This is the comfort the author gives to Christians under actual persecution, not that suffering is not real, or a promise that it won't be too bad. No, the comfort promises joy *in the midst of suffering,* because it is a sharing of Christ's suffering. (Ch. 4:13.) In his resurrection he has become " the Shepherd and Guardian of your souls " (ch. 2:25). As such he will lead the Christians to their glorious destiny: " And when the chief Shepherd is manifested you will obtain the unfading crown of glory " (ch. 5:4).

Christ's way through suffering to glory is the way of the Christian pilgrimage, and as glory was the end of his way, so it will be the end of the way for the Christian. " Rejoice in so far as you share Christ's sufferings, that you may also rejoice and be glad when his glory is revealed." (Ch. 4:13.) The pilgrims do not march through the world as a defeated caravan of displaced persons. As refugees, they are the people of God singing a song of victory that the world must hear: " You are a chosen race, a royal priesthood, a holy nation, God's own people, that you may declare the wonderful deeds of him who called you out of darkness into his marvelous light " (ch. 2:9).

CHAPTER 7 | *The Risk of Allegiance*

THE REVELATION focuses our attention on circumstances taking place about twenty years prior to those described in I Peter. The scene is western Asia Minor, the main center of Christianity at that time. After the destruction of Jerusalem in A.D. 70, many Jewish Christians had left Palestine and had migrated to Asia Minor. Among them, according to early tradition, was John the apostle, to whom this book is usually ascribed. Yet the author never hints that he was an apostle. This John (ch. 1:1, 4, 9) is a prophet and confessor, exiled for his confession of Christ by the Roman Emperor Domitian (A.D. 81–96), to Patmos, a small island a few miles off the coast of Asia Minor. Here on " the Lord's day " (ch. 1:10), when the churches on the mainland were celebrating the Lord's resurrection in their worship service, John united himself with them in spirit. The earthly liturgy of the church was suddenly transformed into a heavenly vision in which he was given to see the victory of the Lamb of God over all forces of history.

The Revelation is a very difficult book. Its own uncompromising attitude — " because you are . . . neither cold nor hot, I will spew you out of my mouth " (ch. 3:16) — is reflected in the history of its interpretation. No book of the New Testa-

ment has received either such acceptance or such rejection, and
that even from earliest times. In many circles, especially sec-
tarian ones, it occupies a central place for faith, whereas in
others it is ignored as an obscure book or rejected as sub-
Christian and revengeful. What indeed can we do with all
the confusing imagery and the series of seemingly unending
and often contradictory visions? What confusion has been
caused by the applications of its numbers and visions to specific historical persons! Practically every outstanding heretic or
politician has been declared the " harlot " (ch. 17:1) or the
" beast " (ch. 13:18), and many a pseudo-prophet has established
the date of the end of the world on the basis of its mysterious
sign, the number *666* (v. 18). So most of us are happy to ignore
The Revelation, except possibly for a few isolated sentences
taken out of context. Yet The Revelation is a peculiar book in
that we cannot understand any of its parts unless we have
caught a glimpse of the unity of the book and its total drive.

LITERARY STRUCTURE

Characteristic of The Revelation is a rather puzzling combination of unity and variety. The variety is due to the great
number of individual, isolated visions and images that are so
frustrating to the reader. Images seem to contradict one another. The seven lampstands, for instance, refer at one time
to the seven churches (ch. 1:20), then again they stand for
God's universal power (v. 13). Likewise, the scenery is inconsistent. John stands now at the threshold of heaven (chs. 1:12;
15:1; 19:11), then again at the border of the sea (ch. 12:17). It
is a mistake to be deceived by this feature of the book, for the
reader is not meant to pause at any one image and to analyze
it rationally. We are dealing here with a visionary. This is a
picture book, the pictures of which pass in a swift rush before

the reader. Only in their total impact do they communicate a sense of unity.

The number 7 is the holy and perfect number of apocalyptic literature, since it denotes divine totality. Although it is a traditional number and serves as the formative principle of many apocalypses, it is carried through in The Revelation with logical consistency. There are seven lampstands (ch. 1:12), seven spirits before God's throne (ch. 4:5), seven stars in the hands of Christ (ch. 1:16), seven eyes and seven horns of the Lamb (ch. 5:6), and so forth. But, more significantly, the book itself is divided into seven parts, as the outline will show. The main part of the book (chs. 4:1 to 21:5) is divided into seven visions, each of which is again subdivided into seven parts. To complete the arrangement of sevens, the main part in its turn is surrounded by seven letters to churches in Asia Minor (chs. 2; 3) and by seven visions of hope (chs. 21:5 to 22:7).

This symmetric unity does not merely constitute a series of unrelated visions, but is conceived in a dynamic rhythm, which is essential to the understanding of the book. The tempo of events described in the book is matched by the dynamic composition. Tension and suspense build up time and again. This happens especially because of preludes and interludes, which break the onrush of occurrences and momentarily breathe absolute calmness and liturgical dignity (as in chs. 7:17; 10:1 to 11:14; 11:15-18; 15:3-4).

The composition gives expression to the main theme of the book: the characterization of the Christian hope. The impatient, longing cry of the martyrs, " O Sovereign Lord, holy and true, how long before thou wilt judge and avenge our blood on those who dwell upon the earth? " (ch. 6:10), is communicated to the reader by the suspense of the composition. A series of events unrolls before our eyes, becoming ever more

The Church Faces the World

tense and yet seemingly endless. The first series of seven rolls off — the seven seals (chs. 6; 7). We expect the climax, but the seventh seal bursts open into another series of seven — the seven trumpets (chs. 8 to 14); and again the seventh trumpet bursts open into the series of the seven bowls (chs. 15; 16). Like a rocket in fireworks, bursting open in ever-new formations, the dramatic tension of The Revelation moves toward its ever-suspended climax.

This climax is the appearance of the Son of Man in ch. 14. From this point the outcome is plain: the judgment of God becomes manifest ever more threateningly, until finally Satan is bound and thrown into the abyss. The millennium arrives, and finally the heavenly Jerusalem appears on earth. Just as the movement *toward* the climax is characterized by the increasing enmity of the world, climaxing in the appearance of the beasts (ch. 13), so the section after ch. 14 points to an increasing judgment, climaxing in the destruction of all Satanic powers and God's final victory.

We may show this structure, so important for understanding The Revelation, by means of an outline:

(Heavenly interlude chs. 10:1 to
   11:14)

3. The seventh trumpet: the
   seven visions of the dragon
              chs. 11:15 to 13:18

Climax 4. The seven visions of the Son of
      Man   ch. 14

5. The seven bowls of God's
   wrath   chs. 15; 16

6. The seven visions of Babylon's
   fall   chs. 17:1 to 19:10

7. The seven visions of the end
             chs. 19:11 to 21:4

Fulfillment

  V. The promise   chs. 21:5 to 22:7
  VI. Epilogue   ch. 22:8-19
  VII. Blessing   ch. 22:20-21

LITERARY BACKGROUND

The Revelation belongs to a type of literature that occurs infrequently in the New Testament but is common to the Jewish tradition out of which the New Testament arose. *Apocalyptic literature* (see the discussion of Jewish apocalyptic literature in *The Threshold of Christianity,* by Lawrence E. Toombs, in this series) is a late form of prophecy, which, unlike prophecy, is more concerned with prediction of God's Final Judgment than with the pronouncement of God's judgment in the present. It usually takes the form of a visionary revelation granted to some Old Testament hero of the past, depicting the future history of the world with visions and images. World history will come to its climax in a time of great crisis, according to the apocalyptic writers. It will be the time that heralds the arrival of God's Kingdom and judgment. The announcement of the breaking in on history of God's Kingdom is the content of the Apocalypse (" vision " or " revelation ") — it is the revealing of what was hidden. The revealer adopts the name of a hero of the past to enhance the authority of his revelation, but usually the time of extreme crisis is the time in which he writes. The Revelation is unique among apocalypses in that the author writes under his own name (ch. 1:1, 4, 9).

Apocalyptic writing regularly employed symbolism from the Old Testament prophets and visionary materials. But by the time The Revelation to John was written this had become little more than a conventional way of putting things. It does not necessarily indicate that John actually saw these dreams or visions. They constitute the " furniture " of apocalyptic literature, which is less important than the message expressed through it.

THE CONCERN OF APOCALYPTIC WRITERS

In " revealing " the hidden future and its several stages the apocalyptic writers were dealing with an extremely important issue: the meaning of history. They were theologians of history, attempting to give an answer to the perennial problem of evil in history and of the suffering of the righteous. Would the just God, who elected his people and promised them salvation, be able to vindicate his righteousness in history? Or would he succumb to the stronger powers of evil embodied in the figure of Satan? This question forced itself upon the Jews when events seemed to show that their oppressors, the Syrians or the Romans who occupied and oppressed Israel, were more powerful than the God of creation and election. God's reign seemed remote, withdrawn. Had he abandoned his people? When would he vindicate himself and the people of his choice? The apocalypticists answered: God will reign, and this reign will be established, not by forces operating in history, but by his sudden appearance, in which he will overthrow Satan and his powers, and establish his people in glory on a new earth where " death shall be no more " (Rev. 21:4). There are, then, three outstanding theological topics with which apocalyptic literature is concerned: the meaning of history, the idea of justice, and the truth of election.

The meaning of history. The apocalyptic writers viewed history as moving toward a climax in which it would be cleansed from evil and in which God's dealings with the world would become clear. God would reign visibly over his creation and over those whom he had chosen. History and the world had become so evil that the crisis must be near. God's new world would wipe away the old: " Then I saw a new heaven and a new earth; for the first heaven and the first earth had passed away " (ch. 21:1).

The idea of justice. The climax of history would be the day of reckoning, when God's people would be vindicated. " Behold, the dwelling of God is with men. He will dwell with them, and they shall be his people. . . . But as for the cowardly, the faithless, the polluted, . . . their lot shall be in the lake that burns with fire and brimstone." (Ch. 21:3, 8.) The tremendous powers of evil in history seemed to push God out of his world, for his own people were trampled down by godless, ruthless oppressors. " I saw under the altar the souls of those who had been slain for the word of God and for the witness they had borne; they cried out with a loud voice, ' O Sovereign Lord, holy and true, how long before thou wilt judge and avenge our blood on those who dwell upon the earth?' " (Ch. 6:9-10.) The judgment would see the faithful glorified and their enemies tortured. Justice, then, demanded a redress on the final day of judgment.

The truth of election. God's judgment would seal his election of his people (Israel in the Jewish apocalypses, the church in

The Revelation to John). Israel and the church had been set apart as witnesses of God's power of salvation. This election, manifest in God's new covenant with his people, promised them a special destiny, which would soon be revealed. In summary, then, on the Day of Judgment history would vindicate God as the Almighty Creator, justice would vindicate God as the Holy One, and election would vindicate God as the Redeemer of his people, if they persevered amidst the desperate onslaughts of evil.

Such a meditation on history underlies The Revelation to John. It is couched in the form of a picture book, but under the images lies the all-important issue. Only in a time of crisis do we see what evil can be unfolded in history. In times of normalcy we tend to dismiss the presence of evil in history, since everything is running on a fairly even keel. A time of crisis makes us stop to think about ultimate meaning in history and our role in it. Thus for the believer history becomes the scene of the struggle between God and Satan, and the destiny of history hinges on the outcome of that struggle. In the midst of such a crisis in history The Revelation to John was written.

HISTORICAL SETTING

John's meditation on history and its ultimate meaning is not the product of contemplation at a desk in a study. His is the mind of a participant in a struggle. For he was in exile by the command of the emperor " on account of the word of God and the testimony of Jesus " (ch. 1:9). He was banished from his churches in Asia Minor at the very moment that a life-and-death struggle was at hand between the church and the Roman Empire under the Emperor Domitian (A.D. 81–96).

His involvement in the struggle is evident in the pastoral letters to the seven Asian churches (chs. 1 to 3). In the form of an imperial decree Christ, the Emperor of the church, gives warning and promise. The promise is "to him who conquers"; the warning is against compromise with the ways of the world; and the demand is for constant faithfulness in the face of oncoming persecution. "Be faithful unto death, and I will give you the crown of life." (Ch. 2:10.) The Greek word for "witness" (*martys*) takes on, for the first time in the New Testament, its English meaning "martyr." For those who witness for Christ will do so not only with their lips but with their lives. In this situation the words of warning and comfort are spoken by John. They are words of warning, because those who forsake their first love and make a "deal" with the world belong to it and will be judged with it. They are words of comfort, because the seeming defeat of God's cause in the world is the very token that "the time [of the Kingdom] is near" (ch. 1:3).

The warning is so urgent, because the seer prophesies about an either-or situation. No alternative is left. One belongs either to the number of the sealed of God, the 144,000 (ch. 7:4), or he carries the mark of the beast, the servant of the dragon, Satan (ch. 13). A Christian cannot walk a double way; his decision is absolute. This is especially true in a time when "making deals" with the world means the difference between life and death. But once the warning is understood, the comfort abounds: "They shall hunger no more, neither thirst any more; the sun shall not strike them, nor any scorching heat. For the Lamb in the midst of the throne will be their shepherd, and he will guide them to springs of living water; and God will wipe away every tear from their eyes" (ch. 7:16-17). The comfort pertains especially to the martyrs, those who "have washed their robes and made them white in the blood of the Lamb" (v. 14).

The author speaks about the meaning of history against the extremely concrete problem of the meaning of suffering. For the early church faced a double perplexity: the delay of the *Parousia* was a problem difficult enough to bear, as we have repeatedly seen; but now this delay was coupled with the threat and actuality of persecution. Those destined to be victorious with Christ, who " made us a kingdom, priests to his God and Father " (ch. 1:6), were now subjected to humiliation and suffering, without any outward signs of victory at all. Indeed, for one who has no hope, there is no meaning in history or in suffering. To the apocalyptic author the meaning of history and suffering could only be given by the end of history, by the God who would finally impose his sovereign will on history.

The crisis in history and its suffering was brought about by Domitian's reign. Domitian took himself very seriously as a divine person. Former emperors had allowed divine titles, but on the whole they had restrained the divine terminology. It is reported that Vespasian (A.D. 69–79), the father of Domitian, was quite skeptical about his divine genealogy and joked on his deathbed: " I think I'm about to become a god! " Domitian was different. He had himself officially entitled " God the Lord," not only in the provinces but also in Rome. He loved to be greeted with, " Hail to the Lord's Lord of Lords, highest of the high, Lord of the earth, god of all things " (compare Rev. 17:14; 19:16). Domitian imagined himself an incarnate God in whose hands lay the destiny of the world.

The imperial cult was elaborately propagandized and accompanied with heavy secret-police activity. Domitian had reason to be suspicious about plots against him, for he was hated in the Empire for his absolutism and imperial madness. One contemporary called him the beast from hell sitting in its den and licking blood. Jews and Christians alike were accused of " atheism," because they refused to worship the Roman and imperial gods. In Ephesus and Pergamum the imperial cult was propagated by the " high priest of Asia." John therefore calls

Pergamum the place "where Satan's throne is" (ch. 2:13), referring to the huge altar to Jupiter there. The main liturgy consisted of the yearly festivals, held in the stadium in honor of "the Lord and God" Domitian. Domitian himself sat on a huge throne amidst divine emblems high above the crowds in the circus. These holy games centered around the image of the emperor on his throne, and they made an enormous impact on the crowd.

It was against this background of the deification of the emperor and his absolute claims that the seer of The Revelation saw the inescapable conflict looming. And on Patmos he wrote his revelation in which he made the imperial language refer to God and Christ. The "Lord and God" Domitian was clashing with the true Lord and God, who would soon cause Domitian's Rome to fall.

Special Emphases

The language of The Revelation is one clue to its religious point of view. It is the language of prophecy. John knew that he stood in the line of the Old Testament prophets, who declared the ultimate will of God over all of history. His peculiar language is not only a way to describe contemporary events or one phase of history. These events are seen in an ultimate dimension, which reveals the hidden forces of history for all time. The author placed himself at the end of history to perceive its meaning. And the end of history, notwithstanding the glittering imagery, is not a Utopian projection of the future, nor the grandiose self-deception of a dreamer imagining his revenge to be divinely sanctioned and executed. It is basically nothing more than a poetic and visionary description of that which believers held in faith. The theme of all history after Christ is nothing more than an uncovering of the glory of Jesus Christ. He *has* judged; he *has* redeemed: therefore, he *will* judge and *will* redeem. Therefore, The Revelation opens with the victorious cry: " Behold, he is coming with the clouds, and every eye will see him, every one who pierced him; and all tribes of the earth will wail on account of him. Even so. Amen " (ch. 1:7). Thus the introduction to the main visionary section is opened with the vision of God on his throne and the Lamb (chs. 4 and 5). The Lamb, alone of all creatures on earth, is allowed to open the book with the seals, which is God's hidden plan for history.

The resurrection of Jesus Christ, " the living one " (ch. 1:18), was the center of the early Christian confession. It is repeated in Revelation in the responses and hymns sung by the heavenly court of the twenty-four elders, the angels of God. On the throne of history is the God of history and the Christ depicted in imperial terminology (vs. 12-16), not the emperor on his circus throne. It is before Him, not before the emperor, that the seer falls (v. 17). It is this constant antithesis to the imperial cult that makes The Revelation so exciting. The imperial demonry planned to crush the seemingly insignificant churches and their God. John, however, knew the true Emperor, against whom little Domitian could have no final power.

God, the Almighty Creator and Lord of all nature and history, has determined the beginning of time and will determine its end. He is portrayed as the Holy Majesty who alone decides what will happen but who is never involved in the struggle. He is majestically remote from the cosmic struggle, because he rules it all by his angels or his word. He is never named but is mysteriously referred to as the " one seated on the throne " (ch. 4:2). The remoteness of God in The Revelation is not a remoteness of indifference but one of absolute, cosmic superiority. It is the superiority of the Alpha and Omega, of the One " who is and who was and who is to come " (ch. 1:8). He is the God of time and history, who determines its course and measures the moments for the events to take place.

The seeming confusion of images and happenings is not arbitrary at all, the author means to say. These are all part of God's preconceived plan of salvation, which rolls on according to his will. Similarly, the number of those who are sealed, the 144,000, points to God's sovereign will (ch. 7:4). The number *12,000* (for each of twelve tribes) expresses the multitude of the New Israel — a symbol of God's faithfulness to the believers in the midst of the approaching chaos and destruction. Whom God has sealed for salvation, no one will tear from his hand. The only one who can approach the awesome majesty of God is Christ, the Son. He alone is enthroned in heaven since his resurrection and exaltation (ch. 12:5). Christ is the universal agent of God's plan for history. Thus the "Lamb who was slain" is also the "Lion" (ch. 5:5-6). The crucified Jesus is the exalted Lord, the bright morning star (ch. 22:16), that is, the turning point of history. And now the judgment of the world is handed over to the Lamb. This judgment will only confirm what has already occurred for faith: that since the first Easter all history has stood under the Lordship of Jesus Christ.

As there is an absolute break between Christ and the world, so this break determines the relation between the church and the world. The sealed of God stand over against the ones marked by the beast. (Chs. 13:16 to 14:5.) What divides them is the witness of Jesus Christ. Just as the Lamb gave glory to God and was obedient to him unto death, so the church of the martyrs is obedient to the Lamb. "It is these who follow the Lamb wherever he goes." (Ch. 14:4.) Just as the Lamb has become the victorious Lord of history, so the martyrs will be victorious with him. "Then I looked, and lo, on Mount Zion stood the Lamb, and with him a hundred and forty-four thousand who had his name and his Father's name written on their foreheads." (Ch. 14:1.) In this hope the church endures until the moment when all imperial and demonic "lordships" will be destroyed. And so the church prays: "Amen. Come, Lord Jesus!" (Ch. 22:20.)

$7.95